I0902619

CASEY IRELAND

CHARLOTTESVILLE FOOD

A HISTORY OF EATING LOCAL IN JEFFERSON'S CITY

Foreword by JED VERITY

AMERICAN PALATE

Published by American Palate
A Division of The History Press
Charleston, SC 29403
www.historypress.net

Copyright © 2014 by Casey Ireland
All rights reserved

First published 2014

Manufactured in the United States

ISBN 978.1.62619.027.6

Library of Congress CIP data applied for.

Notice: The information in this book is true and complete to the best of our knowledge. It is offered without guarantee on the part of the author or The History Press. The author and The History Press disclaim all liability in connection with the use of this book.

All rights reserved. No part of this book may be reproduced or transmitted in any form whatsoever without prior written permission from the publisher except in the case of brief quotations embodied in critical articles and reviews.

For my parents and sister, lovers of good meals and good books.

Contents

Foreword

A few months ago, I went to Portland, Maine, to visit family and friends. Over truffled mac and cheese with a massive glistening pillow of lobster meat on top, my cousin asked me if the farm-to-table movement was as strong in Charlottesville as it was in Portland. I nodded vigorously and told her that *Forbes* magazine had referred to us as the "locavore capital of the world" and that we've also long enjoyed the honor of having more restaurants per capita than anywhere else in the country. At this, the locals at the table let out a collective guffaw. Portland, they said, is well known to have the most restaurants per capita in the country, and the local food movement is not really even a "movement" there because it's the way it's always been. We all took sips of our locally produced pale ales and cabernets and smiled tight smiles at each other.

Reflecting on this later, I decided that both of us must be wrong. Surely there are more restaurants per capita in New York City than in either Portland or Charlottesville. And what are the chances that this local food craze sweeping the nation started in one of our small towns? Some quick Googling revealed that the current title-holder of "most restaurants per capita" is actually Juneau, Alaska, and that there is no consensus whatsoever about the origins of this modern incarnation of the local food movement (though Michael Pollan and Joel Salatin are surely founding fathers, with the latter giving central Virginia an edge over Portland, if I may be so bold).

So why are we sparring over mac and cheese, trying to claim some small victory in this local food arena for our little towns?

Until recently, my wife and I ran a restaurant reviews and food news blog in Charlottesville. We had hoped it would become a place for people to have conversations about food, and it did, but the character of those conversations was more often belligerent than convivial. How can you possibly think this restaurant is good/bad? How can you claim to know anything about food given that you've never been professionally trained? And, most pertinently, why would you patronize an establishment that makes no effort to source its ingredients locally?

It was this last question that hinted at an answer to the earlier question. Any issues of pragmatism wrapped up in the local food movement—fresher produce, support for the local economy, reduction of energy consumption by shortening distances between producers and consumers—have been moralized in the extreme, glorifying those who source and eat their ingredients locally and vilifying the rest.

To an extent, this is not surprising. Energy and the economy are powerfully charged, highly politicized issues. But it goes deeper than that. "Local" has come to be a synonym for other values as well. "Healthy" is one. We're worried that food corporations are more concerned about the bottom line than our bodies, piping in all kinds of chemical preservatives and flavor enhancers to make sure we buy what they sell, such that it feels wiser to eat a local biscuit with local bacon than a corporate salad with foreign fruit. Is it actually healthier to do so? Maybe, maybe not. In the paraphrased words of one of our readers, "If I'm going to go prematurely, I'll take a heart attack while eating a local breakfast sandwich over cancer from a fast-food salad any day of the week!"

This points to another modern synonym of "local," which is "trustworthy." Local farmers could be engaging in all kinds of sadistic, immoral practices just around the bend, but we trust that they're not. They're our neighbors and friends. Surely they're looking out for us more than the faceless executives just trying to make a buck. Right?

"Slow" is another one. Many people talk about the "Slow Food movement" and the "local food movement" in the same breath. In this age of fast food—and "fast casual"—and instantaneous communication with people around the world, we are feeling agile but fatigued, connected but disconnected. Local food promises old(er)-fashioned techniques, fewer ingredients, a simpler and purer experience, with that guy over there who has some good chickens and that family over there with all the goat cheese-producing goats. Pull up a chair, my friend, and let me get you a plate of food. We'll drink a beer from the brewery right around the corner and talk about old times.

Putting aside issues of whether fast-food salads really are carcinogenic, whether local farmers really care less about making money than corporate execs and all the other complex dynamics at play here, we can see in the good-natured debate between Portland locals and Charlottesville locals a contraction of the ever-expanding universe. We have now collectively realized the insane dream of being able to video chat with someone in the Himalayas in real-time, both of us drinking a Coke and eating chicken McNuggets. The spectacle of brand colonialism—walking off a rickety plane in the middle of nowhere in a far-off country to see a Coke umbrella—has lost its luster, if it ever had any. The thing that is special about us is the thing you can't get anywhere else. The people, the food and drink, the history of this place and the experiences to be had right here and now. These are the knowable things, the raw materials of our very being, and they can't be bought or sold anywhere else.

—Jed Verity
Charlottesville, Virginia
November 2013

Acknowledgements

This book is the result of the encouragement and opportunities given to me by Jed Verity and Erin Malec of Mas to Millers. Their guidance, experience and general know-how has been an indispensable part of the book-writing process. Greg and Debbie Ireland, Chelsea Ireland and Kevin Haney have given me incredible support—they've functioned as sounding boards, proofreaders, marketers and cheerleaders. Kevin's photography, eye for detail and unwavering dedication have been essential to the completion of this work and my sanity as an author.

The food community in Charlottesville is a knowledgeable and enthusiastic one. Without the backing of local farmers, retailers, restaurateurs and craftspeople, this text would have no stories to tell. Sincere thanks to Peter Hatch of Monticello for his easy wisdom; his vibrant personal background and incredible knowledge base proved integral to the historical foundations of this book. Every one of the individuals interviewed has been kind, resourceful and eager to help. I am forever grateful for the conversations, farm visits and friendships granted to me by this group of food-minded individuals during the past year.

Introduction

The local food scene in Charlottesville has taken off by leaps and bounds within the past twenty years. The once-scrubby City Market has morphed into a veritable Mecca of seasonal foodstuffs; the Boar's Head Inn, one of the only places to offer simple fine dining with regional flavor twenty years ago, is now one of many stellar restaurants putting out quality meals with local ingredients. Gabriele Rausse, local vintner and director of gardens and grounds at Monticello, tells a story of fancy dinners flown in from New York and frozen baguettes from Washington, D.C., purchased at Foods of All Nations.

Twenty years ago, gourmet retail standbys like Feast! had not yet burst onto the scene; the luxurious handmade lasagna sheets of Mona Lisa Pasta, raspberry jam of Agriberry Farm and delicate and precious quail eggs from Down Branch Farm were nonexistent during this period. While marked by an educated, somewhat cosmopolitan population in the city, Charlottesville possessed a food scene that was a far cry from its current luxuriousness today.

What happened over twenty years that led to the creation of such a vibrant, accessible and renowned culinary tradition? Trends in agriculture and cooking, often small in scale, alternative movements spearheaded by freethinkers and discontents, have trickled into the mountains and valleys of central Virginia from California, New York and the urban South. The rise of organic agriculture, farm-to-table eating and farmers' markets have all been absorbed with great success into the existing foodways of the Charlottesville area.

Wendell Berry, a founder of the organic food movement, proclaimed in 2008, "'Organic' has become a label, as it was destined to be."[1] To Berry,

Johnson grass at Timbercreek Organics. *Photo by Casey Ireland.*

"organic" as a descriptor has become "a completely worthless word now. It has been perverted to suit the needs of industrial agriculture."[2] In the wake of organic's demise, a new label has appeared in the texts of Joel Salatin and the farms of the Piedmont: "beyond organic." USDA-designated conceptions of organic growing, with their focus on fertilizers, feed and chemicals, remain an inadequate way of labeling a product influenced by permaculture, heritage breeds and biomimicry. The holistic, ecologically minded concept of "beyond organic" eating and farming has begun to fill the niches left by the large-scale successes of businesses like Horizon Organics and Earthbound Farms.

Organic, as a descriptor and a USDA-approved label, has begun to lose its monopoly over the food markets of health-conscious consumers. The imported California organic tomato, trucked across the country with a price tag to make up for its long transit, has begun to fall out of favor against the lumpy, lobed charm of a backyard plant purchased from Monticello's garden store. The aisles of "natural" peanut butters, Australian honey and Vermont cheddar grow empty as consumers begin to seek closer, homegrown solutions to their allergies and preferences. To Charlottesville diners and cooks, the little green label of USDA Organic, once a revolution in its own right, has become less attractive than the farmers' market, the CSA pickup and the roadside stand. Locavore eating has captured the city's imagination and has made for some of the most memorable meals, colorful characters and captivating stories the commonwealth has to offer.

Chapter 1

Monticello and Thomas Jefferson

The Origin of (Heirloom) Species

Putting Charlottesville on the Map

How has Charlottesville, a town of only forty-three thousand people, made such an indelible mark on the culinary landscape of the United States? From the winemaking dreams of Thomas Jefferson to the pasture pens of Joel Salatin, this white-columned city has fostered the careers of several of the nation's most influential innovators of and experts on food and drink. How have the mountains and hills of central Virginia yielded such a bounty of restaurateurs and vintners, not to mention such demanding consumers? We may frame these questions better by mapping the area's historical and geographic boundaries. The red clay soil underneath the ruins at Barboursville Vineyards or the gnarled apple trees left over from Jeffersonian intrepidness tell a story as rich and vibrant as the land itself.

Charlottesville is the county seat of Albemarle County, but it remains an independent city within the geographic confines of Albemarle. The rural counties of Greene, Fluvanna and Nelson share borders with Albemarle County, connected by a network of major U.S. highways and smaller route systems. These four counties and the city of Charlottesville combined as a Metropolitan Statistical Area (MSA) host a population of a mere 200,000, a blip on the overall state population of 8 million.[3] The 1,700 square miles that make up the Charlottesville MSA parallel or cross the Blue Ridge Mountains and cozy up to rural streams or the Rivanna River, an offshoot of the James. The climate is humid sub-tropical with four full seasons and considerable

Zach Miller holding a blue chicken egg laid by an Araucana chicken. *Photo by Casey Ireland.*

precipitation throughout the year, though a period from late spring to early fall sees the most rainfall. Relatively cold winters are a mainstay of the area, particularly in the high altitudes of the Blue Ridge. The yearly averages of twenty-two inches of snow and 35.9-degree Januaries contrast with hot, muggy summers with frequent highs over 90.0 degrees.[4] This is a place of full, developed seasons, of crisp fall days and pebbly mountain streams. It's a landscape ripe for peach orchards, roadside produce stands, cideries and heritage pork raising.

Charlottesville as a metropolitan area, university town and corporate center takes up a mere 10.3 square miles of these 1,700 square miles of land.[5] Its streets, neighborhoods and buildings are filled with a surprisingly wide variety of people from different nationalities, ethnicities and backgrounds. The University of Virginia draws professors and staff as well as students to the area; UVA itself and UVA Medical Center are the two largest employers in the city, offering more than thirteen thousand jobs to local residents.[6] The International Rescue Committee's office in Charlottesville resettles an average of two hundred refugees a year, offering them shelter and sustenance as well as job training and housing opportunities.[7] The growing Muslim contingent, Bhutanese families from Nepal and Tibetan monks have made space for themselves among traditional Charlottesville communities and neighborhoods, making the city more diverse year after year.

Even raw data like these statistics about Charlottesville's population and geography gives some insight into what makes the area such a hotbed of agricultural, culinary and multicultural progress. The long growing season, humidity and topography of Charlottesville's surrounding counties make the land well suited to a variety of agricultural products. Peppery-smelling field greens, long sheaves of rainbow chard and viscerally red beets are a sample of the produce available at the farmers' market almost nine months out of the year. Snowy January evenings are perfect for hearty stews of local beef, eating thin shavings of Virginia-raised prosciutto and making sauces with the last Mason jar of August's tomatoes. Fresh-caught mountain trout ends up on the plates of world-class chefs lured to the area by foraged mushrooms and first-rate teachers. UVA's touted position as the second-best public school in the nation draws in intellectuals and students who then, when they combine passions for taste and for learning, take root in a restaurant loft above the Downtown Mall or a patch of earth in Monticello's gardens.

Eating with Thomas Jefferson

We modern culinary enthusiasts are not the first to have planted grapes, battled farmyard pests or cured sides of pork in this region. The beauty and ecological richness of Charlottesville and the surrounding counties led Thomas Jefferson to make his home at Monticello hundreds of years before homesteading came on board as a lifestyle choice. Our nation's third president has the joint honor of being a founding foodie as well as a founding father.[8] In the Charlottesville area, Jefferson is as famous for his experimental gardening efforts as he is for the Louisiana Purchase. Visitors to Monticello can tour flower, vegetable and fruit gardens re-created in painstaking detail from historical clues about the originals. A love of both imported wine and backyard cucumbers marks Thomas Jefferson as the original Charlottesville epicurean.

Born in 1743 in Shadwell, Virginia, now a part of Albemarle County, Jefferson inherited five thousand acres of local farmland upon turning twenty-one.[9] A deep-rooted love of learning and ceaseless quest for knowledge marked Jefferson's intellectual life as well as his active gardening and horticultural efforts as a young man. A study of his *Garden Book*, a combination of horticultural diary, letter collection and sketchbook, reveals that Jefferson was gardening at twenty-three and recording the blooming dates of local wildflowers. Later deciding "the greatest service which can be rendered any country is to add a useful plant to its culture,"[10] it perhaps comes as no surprise that Jefferson spent a considerable portion of his pre-political youth laying the groundwork for the horticultural and culinary interests that so define both his presidency and personal life.

The "author" of a developing post-colonial country, Jefferson's epicurean and political leanings often took on an attitude of regional insularity and fierce independence. During the War of 1812, Jefferson shared a sentiment of self-sufficiency not unlike a modern conception of homesteading. Sounding positively anti-establishmentarian, Jefferson acknowledges, "We must endeavor to make every thing we want within ourselves, and have as little intercourse as possible with Europe in its present demoralised state."[11] The demoralization of Europe, it seems, can be transferred from the realm of politics to the realm of culinary consumption. To import European foodstuffs is, to Jefferson, to further support an antagonistic and outdated political and cultural entity. Part of Jefferson's political platform, as well as his personal ideology, was the construction of a morally clean, democratically developed and unpretentious alternative to the static failures of the Old World. The creation of a purer source of political power went hand-in-hand with an interest in promoting more direct food sources, a development that was to occur right in Jefferson's backyard.

As an adult, Jefferson provided one of his best-known contributions to Monticello and American agriculture in the form of his extraordinarily plentiful vegetable garden. Historian Peter J. Hatch calls Jefferson a "seedy evangelist," referring to his garden as "an Ellis Island of vegetables."[12] This one-thousand-foot-long enclosed space held a remarkable 330 varieties of 89 species of vegetables and herbs and 170 fruit varieties.[13] One can get a sense for Jefferson's favorite vegetables by the frequency of plantings rather than mere epistolary enthusiasm; the English pea appears to have been the president's most favorite vegetable based on the number of plantings, the amount of garden space allotted to their growth and the textual description of his "pea contests" held with neighboring horticultural enthusiasts.[14] If one were to take Jefferson's gushing remarks about the taste of the Marseilles fig or the values of an olive as concrete evidence of utter devotion, both the actual layout of his garden as well as its modern reconfiguration would have looked much different—and arguably would have been possible only in a different clime.

The layout, design and tending of the vegetable garden proved crucial to its success as an experimental horticultural playground. Jefferson's decision to carve the one-thousand-foot-long terrace from the southeastern slope of Monticello resulted in the creation of a microclimate, or a pocket of distinct atmospheric conditions existing within a larger zone.[15] The man-made terrace traps the sunshine, which leads to the earlier production of crops and an extended growing season. The slight elevation of the estate deterred harmful frost, as cold air forces warm air to drift upward during winter nights.[16] Jefferson's use of manure as fertilizer, careful study and manipulation of roots and seeds and general watchful eye provided his gardens with basic structural integrity and strong foundations.

A crucial facet of the garden's success was Jefferson's interest in procuring and distributing seed varieties. When certain crops and plant varieties failed in central Virginia, geologist William Maclure informed Jefferson, "Sufficient attention has not been paid in the choice of seeds to the previous habits of the vegetable depending much on the nature of the Climate and perhaps something on the soil."[17] Though Jefferson did tailor his garden to the weather and geography of central Virginia, his delight in acquiring new, even exotic, species of plants never failed. Jefferson's correspondences reveal his excitement about procuring new varieties and, even more so, his delight at sharing seeds of his own. The Lewis and Clark expedition offered an incredible variety of new plant species "peculiar to the countries [Lewis] has visited" for Jefferson to examine and send out to friends.[18] Indeed, such horticultural excitement over these newly discovered samples led Bernard McMahon, one of Jefferson's chief gardening associates from Philadelphia, to "painfully" ask Jefferson for seeds.[19] Though Jefferson might be "so much occupied with the important affairs of the Nation," his "goodness" allowed McMahon to "procure some seeds of the indigenous plants of the western parts of America" after all.[20]

Given the complex, often opaque naming system Jefferson employed—identifying plants by the person who gave him the seed, a physical characteristic or place of origin—it's not surprising that the Center for Historic Plants, an offshoot of Monticello's gardening restoration, and Monticello itself have encountered difficulty in placing, naming and uncovering many of the species about which Jefferson wrote. But seed-sleuthing aside, the work of naming, trading and raising unique and heritage plant species continues on today in the Charlottesville area. The Heritage Harvest Festival seeks to continue the seed-trading work of Jefferson in a modern context, albeit in a more crowd-friendly manner. Organized in 2007 by Ira Wallace, the owner of Southern Exposure Seed Exchange, the annual event began at the Center for Historic Plants at Jefferson's Tufton Farm and has since been relocated to Monticello's West Lawn—a view at which Jefferson would have gazed while working in his study.[21] The Heritage Harvest Festival offers lectures, workshops and general educational programs on the arts and joys of small farming, gardening and sustainable living. Events such as "Monticello Herbs & Their Uses" or "Thomas Jefferson & Natural History Woodland Walk" were clearly designed with Monticello's former inhabitant in mind and would have undoubtedly been of considerable interest to him.

While some interested in homesteading and horticulture may take their cues from the early days of Monticello's gardens, those more invested in the culinary arts may take inspiration from the meals created with the gardens' bounty. Jefferson has attained the recent accolade of founding foodie for numerous reasons, with the rumored creation of macaroni and cheese being among them. One of the first American recipes for ice cream is in Thomas Jefferson's cursive handwriting; the eggy custard that he describes doesn't seem dissimilar from the ingredients listed on the side of a container from Wirtz, Virginia's Homestead Creamery. His penchant for foreign delicacies as well as homegrown produce has been well documented by modern journalists and Jefferson's contemporaries. If Thomas Jefferson's horticultural correspondences and widely sourced seed collections indicate a tension between the local and the nonnative, a joint interest in the exotic and everyday, records of his meals and general palate confirm these complementary gastronomic concerns.

Jefferson may have loved his "tomatas" and homegrown English peas, but he also possessed a taste for Parmesan cheese and good Bordeaux. In letters and reports, Jefferson extolled the virtues of the olive tree, a fruit that he experienced during a voyage to the Mediterranean. He was bitterly disappointed when the trees did not grow well in South Carolina and Georgia.[22] His difficulty in getting "the richest gift of heaven" to succeed in Monticello gardens or in the humid flatness of the southern coast foreshadowed his continued difficulty with getting American soil and climate to cooperate with coveted foreign seeds.[23] Though Jefferson often sought alternatives to these costly imported goods, attempts at locally produced alternatives often fared poorly. Jefferson's attempts to use sesame seeds, "among the most valuable acquisitions our country has ever made," for salad oil likely met with the same frustrated lack of success as the southern olive trees.[24]

Ultimately, the food costs of both his homegrown and imported ventures indicate Jefferson's culinary interests to be dependent on his considerable disposable income. Jefferson spent almost $10,000 in wine and groceries during his first year as president ($3,000 on wine and $6,500 on foodstuffs); Jefferson's yearly salary was $25,000. In comparison, Meriwether Lewis was paid a mere $500 as his entire salary for the westward expedition.[25] While trips to Paris and well-developed state dinners were part and parcel of Jefferson's political career, the French chefs he hired, Italian wine he imported and sesame seed presses he purchased indicate that Jefferson's more developed culinary pursuits were dependent on, and perhaps resulted from, his wealth.

What exactly constituted this rich Jeffersonian diet? To a modern reader, Jefferson's dietary preferences read like a cross between semi-vegetarianism and the everything-in-moderation diet of continental Europeans. In an 1819 letter to Dr. Vine Utley, Jefferson describes his diet in no uncertain and rather self-congratulatory terms, expressing a practice of culinary moderation so consistent as to make fellow founding father Benjamin Franklin proud. "I have lived temperately," Jefferson attests, "eating little animal food, and that not as an aliment, so much as a condiment for the vegetables which constitute my principal diet." Jefferson admits to going over his doctor's recommendation of one and a half glasses of wine a day, drinking almost five glasses if entertaining, yet maintains that his choice in lighter wines negates the potential excess. "Ardent wines and ardent spirits" never accompany Jefferson's meals; rather, "malt liquors and cider are [his] table drinks."[26]

Multicultural Influences in Monticello's Kitchen

The style and cuisine of Jefferson's meals reflect the various regional and national influences on Jefferson himself. Peter Hatch attests, "The western traditions of gardening 'in England, France, Spain, the Mediterranean' were blended into a dynamic and unique Monticello cookery through the influence of emerging colonial European, native American, slave, Creole and southwestern vegetables."[27] Recipes exist in the hands of Jefferson and his family for okra stew, fresh pea soup and sweet potato biscuits, dishes that combine Old World food traditions with startlingly new and fresh ingredients. Luckily for Jefferson, the mix of cuisines, flavors and ingredients seldom resulted in an upset stomach. Jefferson brags to have "been blest with organs of digestion which accept and concoct, without ever murmuring, whatever the palate chooses to consign to them."[28]

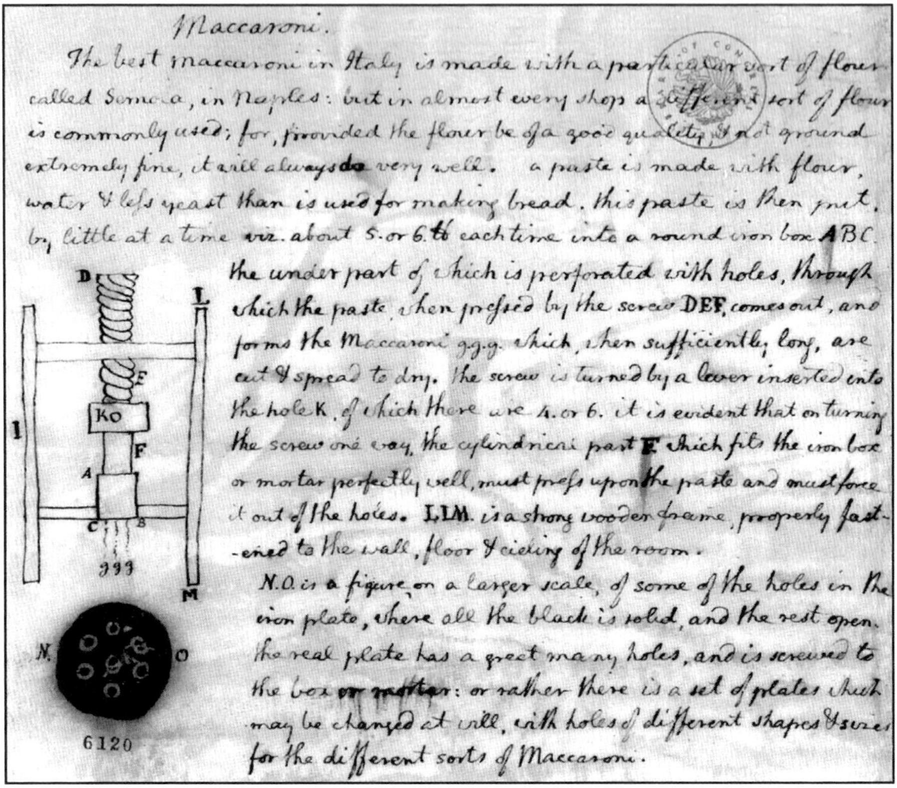

Maccaroni.

The best maccaroni in Italy is made with a particular sort of flour called Semola, in Naples: but in almost every shop a different sort of flour is commonly used; for, provided the flour be of a good quality & not ground extremely fine, it will always do very well. a paste is made with flour, water & less yeast than is used for making bread. this paste is then put, by little at a time viz. about 5. or 6 lb each time into a round iron box ABC. the under part of which is perforated with holes, through which the paste when pressed by the screw DEF, comes out, and forms the Maccaroni g.g.g. which, when sufficiently long, are cut & spread to dry. the screw is turned by a lever inserted into the hole K, of which there are 4. or 6. it is evident that on turning the screw one way, the cylindrical part E which fits the iron box or mortar perfectly well, must press upon the paste and must force it out of the holes. LLM. is a strong wooden frame, properly fastened to the wall, floor & cieling of the room.

N.O. is a figure, on a larger scale, of some of the holes in the iron plate, where all the black is solid, and the rest open. the real plate has a great many holes, and is screwed to the box ~~or mortar~~: or rather there is a set of plates which may be changed at will, with holes of different shapes & sizes for the different sorts of Maccaroni.

A blueprint for Jefferson's pasta machine. *Courtesy of the Library of Congress.*

Though it is commonly thought that Julia Child introduced the United States to French haute cuisine, Jefferson's 1784 visit to Paris might be just as responsible. Like any Jeffersonian accommodations worth their salt, culinary delights at his home began in connection with accessible gardens. Jefferson resided in the Hôtel de Langeac, a fashionable *maison* on the even more fashionable Champs Elysées, for four years during his station as minister to the court of Versailles.[29] Like his previous accommodation, the Hôtel Landron, the Hôtel de Langeac had an English garden on-site. How large a factor these small garden spaces in the middle of urban businesses played in Jefferson's choice of Parisian quarters is unknown. However, his insistence on a house with a garden when moving to Philadelphia in the 1790s indicates that his love of recreational horticulture was likely a factor in his accommodation choice in Paris.[30]

While Jefferson attended to government appointments and matters of state, his cook, James Hemings, attended to the kitchen of a caterer named

Combeaux. A mixed-race slave with reputed blood ties to Jefferson's wife, Martha Wayles Skelton Jefferson, Hemings returned to Monticello after his stay in Paris, despite the fact he could have remained as a free man, given that slavery was illegal in France at the time. During his stay, Hemings learned both the art of French cooking as well as the language itself so well that Jefferson felt confident serving Hemings's creations to French dignitaries and people of influence.[31] Hemings advanced enough in both language and cooking skills to earn the lofty title of *chef de cuisine* at the Hôtel de Langeac.[32]

The cultural and culinary complexity of this situation is quintessentially Jeffersonian: an African American cook learns French cuisine at Jefferson's request, only to return to Virginia to replicate his learnings with the bounty of Monticello's own gardens and some choice imported materials. Jefferson maintained his penchant for French cuisine even after Hemings had been granted his freedom and moved to Baltimore. Edith Fossett cooked for Jefferson in the president's house as well as in post-retirement Monticello in a similarly inspired manner. Daniel Webster perhaps described Jefferson's meals, as cooked by Fossett, best as "in half Virginian, half French style, in good taste and abundance."[33]

The influence of a distinctly continental brand of epicureanism touched Jefferson's palate in more ways than on the plate. Jefferson's appreciation of wine and his particular preferences also evolved after his 1784 visit to France. Prior to this journey, Jefferson had enjoyed the port and Madeira characteristic of Anglo-American wine consumption. Upon returning from his 1784 trip to Paris, Jefferson brought almost seven hundred bottles of wine with him.[34] Recalling the effects his Parisian stay had on his developing palate, Jefferson noted, "The taste of this country [was] artificially created by our long restraint under the English government to the strong wines of Portugal and Spain."[35] Jefferson's preference for lighter French and Italian wines became as much a political statement as personal preference. Following the American Revolution, his favoring of *nebbiolo* and Champagne wines offered a revolution of taste, a way of creating a new oenological heritage.

The depth of his interest in and love of gardening, food and wine does not mean that Jefferson's ardor for epicurean pursuits had no practical, physical limitations. Jefferson was not a cook himself and had only recreational contact with his gardens and food production at Monticello. Many of the vegetables that fed the household were purchased from slave households by Jefferson rather than the products of his gardens. Jefferson may have planted seeds upon seeds of prickly-seeded spinach or tended to the lime-green fruits of the Marseilles fig, but it was the potatoes, corn and onions of Monticello's African

Americans that made up the bulk of Monticello's food offerings. The demands of politics, myriad personal interests and limited leisure time made Jefferson's culinary interests as much intellectual pursuits as physical realities.

It is historically problematic to discuss the accomplishments of Jefferson and Monticello without discussing the influence and presence of enslaved workers. Felisa Rogers notes the crucial fact that Jefferson's meals were prepared by slaves, his surplus food needs attended by them and his orchards tended by them. Through the stories told by household records and letters, one may glean a crucial ambivalence in Jefferson's attitude toward slavery and the utility of slaves from a culinary and a cultural standpoint. Jefferson took many seeds and plants, not to mention cooks themselves, from the slave community at Monticello yet considered their own nutritious needs to be on par with those of livestock.

In his *Garden Book*, Jefferson records three farm products that will replace bacon and corn: potatoes, clover and sheep. "The two former to feed every animal on the farm except my negroes, & the latter to feed them, diversified with rations of salted fish and molasses, both of them wholesome, agreeable, & cheap articles of food."[36] The "animal feed" for Jefferson's slaves is made of hearty yet "cheap" material; the elaborate French dinners James Hemings designed were not to be his own cuisine, no matter the occasion. The sesame seeds with which Jefferson made salad oil, the okra in his stews and the hands executing French meals in his kitchens are a testament to the influence of African Americans on Jefferson's gardening and culinary ventures. The image of "veteran aids," or old slaves, tending Monticello's vegetable garden are as important to visualize for a complete historical assessment of the time as the image of a supervising Jefferson himself.

This impression of Monticello as an experimental playground filled with myriad pleasures, frustrations and ethnic influences is remarkably similar to the reality of the plantation today. The land and gardens in which Jefferson took so much joy have been returned to a vision of their former glory, thanks to the intrepid research and hard work of the Thomas Jefferson Foundation (TJF). A visitor at Monticello today can walk through the vineyards, fruitery and vegetable gardens to see plants with their original names in a layout similar to what originally existed. However, Monticello's current interest in—and successes with—historical accuracy has been somewhat recent and implemented by several major players in the preservation area. Just as Jefferson seems almost before his time in supporting a local, agrarian economy, those involved with the TJF are interested in making sure his ideals are still reflected in a twenty-first-century setting.

Jefferson's Inheritance in Charlottesville and Monticello

Before Peter Hatch, a wild-haired import from Chapel Hill via Detroit, came on board as superintendent of grounds at Monticello in 1977, the gardens and grounds were in a state of misuse and disarray. No single stone of Jefferson's original garden walls remained; the South Orchard did not exist, nor did Jefferson's vineyards or nurseries. Of the original vegetable garden space, 40 percent had been turned into a parking lot, while flowers filled the rest. Floral horticulture was the main focus of the garden and grounds operation when Hatch arrived, using various flower gardens to provide the house with stunning arrangements yet neglecting the more historically accurate uses of the space. Hatch notes, "At the time, the Thomas Jefferson Foundation (henceforth TJF) was a simpler organization, and Monticello more of a shrine." Hatch, who retired from Monticello in April 2012, firmly believes the estate, through the evolution of the TJF, has become "an activist educational and preservation institution." The year 1977 proved a landmark for both Hatch and the TJF; Hatch's goal of using the landscape to display

Peter Hatch and some lima bean plants. *Photo by Kevin Haney.*

and educate visitors on Thomas Jefferson's various interests and aspects was made a reality when the board of trustees committed to recapturing and reconstituting much of the Jefferson-era landscape such as the Grove, the fruit and vegetable gardens, roadways, fences and tree plantings.[37]

Numerous modern add-ons such as roadways and the aforementioned parking lot had to be scraped away before Hatch could begin his painstaking restoration. With the help of then-director Dan Jordan, Hatch began the process of sifting through Jefferson's letters, memos and journal entries to find clues as to the original layout, design and makeup of Jefferson's gardens. Stains in the red clay soil demarcated where fence posts, fruit trees and garden pavilions once lay. With answers in the soil and in Jefferson's textual artifacts, Hatch pieced together the plans for the current layout of the gardens. Meanwhile, an astonishing collection and categorization of heritage herb and vegetable seeds began to take root, created in the image of Jefferson's original seed library by Hatch. The boundaries between garden spaces and natural landscape, Jefferson's era and the present age and old vegetable varieties and new flavors began to blur in a comfortingly complex Jeffersonian fashion at Monticello under Peter Hatch's thirty-four-year tenure.

Ten years later, the restoration of Monticello's gardens and grounds joined with the development of the Center for Historic Plants (henceforth CHP) in 1987. Housed at Tufton Farm, one of Monticello's satellite farms, the CHP was developed as a way to "collect, preserve, and distribute" heirloom and heritage seed varieties such as those planted by Jefferson and catalogued by Hatch. The center takes its residence in an old, converted barn on a beautifully meandering landscape, studded with rose bushes and trellises—and the neighbor's cows. The CHP works closely with Southern Exposure Seed Exchange, the same business that sponsors the Heritage Harvest Festival on Monticello grounds each year. Brown Dutch lettuce, Cherokee purple tomatoes and Marrowfat pea seeds are among the offerings available through the center's shop. In June, visitors to the center can walk through the Léonie Bell Rose Garden with a glass of wine in hand, taking in the rich fragrance of Ruth's pink musk roses with a sip of Gabriele Rausse's Virginia dry rosé.

Like Monticello, the Center for Historic Plants has a wide-reaching influence on issues of historical preservation and education. The CHP has worked with the Lewis Ginter Botanical Garden in Richmond and also the "Paradox of Liberty" exhibit in St. Louis. Lily Fox-Brugière, coordinator for the CHP, helped create a garden that went along with the exhibit for the Gillette Family Garden, a representation of a Monticello slave family's working garden. Growing interest in the influence of African American culture and cuisine on Monticello led to the CHP's involvement with background research and the donation of seeds. According to Fox-Brugière, the slaves at Monticello had the largest, most highly functional gardens instead of Jefferson's more experimental efforts.[38] The CHP's involvement with accurately portraying what plants were grown by slaves and the plants with African American cultural associations that Jefferson grew represents the Thomas Jefferson Foundation's current focus on promoting awareness of our third president's multicultural influences.

Similar to the CHP's participation in national events, the current restoration and educational programs of Monticello have impacted more areas than Monticello's immediate Charlottesville-Albemarle surroundings. Along with the CHP, Monticello has donated seeds to Charlottesville-Albemarle schoolyard gardens and participates in the Heritage Harvest Festival. Peter Hatch's advising role in the creation of Michelle Obama's White House kitchen garden has been documented by everyone from the HGTV Gardens network to the White House's official blog. Thanks to the expertise and advice of Monticello's former superintendent, tennis ball lettuce and Savoy cabbage of Jefferson's preference were planted in the Obamas' own rich spot of earth.

On a more personal and localized note, Hatch admits to a friendly rivalry during his time at Monticello between himself and Dean Norton of Mount Vernon about who was the "better" Virginian: Thomas Jefferson at Monticello or George Washington at Mount Vernon. Excess produce from the vegetable garden goes toward Monticello's café, often stymying workers who know less of purple calabash tomatoes than hothouse imported varieties. Gabriele Rausse, Hatch's successor as director of garden and grounds and famed local, asserts, "The heirloom is wonderful by itself." According to him, "The café is starting to accept the situation" as one outside the typical selections of Kroger and big-box stores "and do something with them." The big thinkers behind Monticello's revitalization can also enjoy the juicy bite of a homegrown summer tomato or the silliness of razzing old friends.

Perhaps Alice Waters's 2012 visit to Monticello best exemplifies the relevance, if not the necessity, of a restored Jeffersonian horticultural space to larger national concerns with sustainable agriculture and food heritage. Waters began her particular brand of no-nonsense, organic and sustainable cooking in Berkeley in 1971, a counterculturally back-to-basics move not unlike her free speech activism. Waters, as a revolutionary California chef, joins forces with Jefferson as a revolutionary gardener in the foreword to

Peter Hatch's esteemed book on Jefferson's gardens, *A Rich Spot of Earth*. Waters urges readers to "reconnect ourselves to the pastoral and self-sufficient tradition that Jefferson built," finding that "nothing is more vital than returning this tradition to the very heart of American culture."[39] Waters and her world-renowned local food pioneer of a restaurant, Chez Panisse, produced a meal for the inner sanctum of Thomas Jefferson Foundation philanthropists. Chesapeake Bay she-crab bisque, milk-fed lamb, vegetable ragout and Monticello honey-based nougat were among the dishes that nourished the guests both physically and ideologically.[40] Ms. Waters told diners to "think of this meal as a slow-food meal [and] absorb some of Jefferson's values—camaraderie, beauty, aliveness, sustainability, generosity."[41] To Waters, cooking at Monticello and eating like Jefferson would inspire even laymen to create cultural monuments of Constitution-size proportions.

Yet visiting Slow Food chefs and heirloom tomatoes in café salads are not the only local, historical culinary ventures on Monticello Mountain. When riding up Route 53 on the way to Monticello, one passes by a hulking, three-story white building with sprawling additions and an old-fashioned charm. This whitewashed façade houses Michie Tavern, a holdover from 1784 that was moved from Earlysville, Virginia, to its current position one mile away from Monticello in 1927. The tavern remained within the Michie family and stayed operational until the 1880s before becoming a private home and then a borderline derelict building. Mrs. Mark Henderson's decision to purchase the tavern as a museum and an antiques display constitutes an early effort in our area to preserve historically—and culinarily—valuable relics from Virginia history.[42]

MICHIE TAVERN: MORE HISTORY ON THE MOUNTAIN

Known around town for its classic fried chicken and all-you-can-eat buffet, Michie Tavern offers early American history in an immediately consumable setting. Events such as the Yuletide Feast, a yearly Christmastime celebration so popular that Michie Tavern doesn't advertise it, showcase the restaurant's joint capacity for making new traditions as well as guarding older ones. Cindy Conte, the marketing director at the restaurant, finds that "as with any historic site, there is a delicate balance to change with the times while staying true to your past."[43] Small menu changes, retail outlets and packages with "partners" Monticello and Ash Lawn–Highland keep Michie Tavern successful in the present. Similar to Monticello and the Center for Historic Plants, Michie Tavern remains interested in educating its visitors in addition to feeding them. It, too, is a Virginia Historic Landmark and remains a famous local example of early preservation efforts in our area. Visitors to Michie Tavern have the option of participating in a tour group or shopping at the General Store, as well as the ability to go get one more side of black-eyed peas and stewed tomatoes.

What does the future look like for Monticello Mountain as a stomping ground for traditional agriculture, newfangled sustainability efforts and epicurean heritage? Gabriele Rausse has taken the reins of seed cataloguing and garden tending from Peter Hatch; his presence at Monticello represents a continuance in the direction of historical rediscovery and educational efforts. A native of Valdagno, Italy, Rausse and his agricultural science degree bring a decidedly European sensibility to the gardens and grounds operation at Monticello, a sensibility with which Jefferson himself would have undoubtedly been enamored. "I'd never seen a can," Rausse laughs, referring to his preservative-free childhood in Italy.[44] A spry sixty-seven, Rausse rivals the records of an elderly Jefferson for best health and attitude at Monticello. "I believe that I am still very healthy because they say 'you are what you eat.' I have a can opener in case someone brings a can as a gift, I can show them I can open it." His love of good vegetables, a life spent out of doors and a deep attachment to olive oil have made Rausse's presence at Monticello positively Jeffersonian.

Like Hatch, Rausse has a primary interest in furthering research and awareness of the different varieties of vegetables, fruits and flowers grown at Monticello. Using the *Garden Book* and the *Farm Book*, Rausse is eager to dig up the original names of plant varieties. In one of his documents, Thomas Jefferson referred to a tomato as a *pomme d'amour*, leading an observer to conceive of the name as a distinct variety. However, *pomme d'amour* was the French name for tomatoes during that period. Rausse uses this instance to distinguish a potential variety from a casual title. When faced with the tomato referred to in Jefferson's log as "large red," Rausse takes note. "To me, it doesn't mean anything, it means that somehow, somebody brought to him a big tomato from the garden," he attests. "I don't think someone would call their son 'big son,' they would give him a name. To me, that tomato should have had a name."[45] Whether recovering lost seed names or planting new vineyards, Rausse and his work at Monticello reflect the same activity, inquisitiveness and forward thinking of his immediate predecessor, Hatch, as well as Jefferson himself.

Monticello's plans for the future are both expansive and charmingly localized. Rausse has expressed interest in making the "Mecca of America" more visible to European travelers. "I always give the example of Italians who come here—they come to New York, they come to Washington, they go to California. What would we have in Virginia?" Rausse asks. "There is so much that is not being told about this area and about Monticello because there is the pressure of other business who prefers to bring them in other places."[46] Rausse's European presence at Monticello will surely engage visitors from other countries as more discussion of Jefferson's multicultural interests takes place. The continued connection between Monticello, Montpelier, Ash Lawn and Michie Tavern will only continue to strengthen the historical and social value of each landmark. The 53/20 Neighborhood Association shows the communal ties between these historic places, with neighboring landmarks along Routes 53 and 20 hosting lunch events together twice yearly. According to Cindy Conte, "It's very informal…It's just neighbors networking, helping one another out (if need be) and keeping one another abreast of any changes that may be taking place in our area." Yearly luncheons, schoolyard garden donations and international flavor are the very things that make Monticello Mountain and its landmarks both local heroes and American Meccas.

From floral arrangements and parking lots to vintage apple trees and heritage lettuce heads, the gardens of Monticello's evolution over the past fifty years represent a victory for North American horticultural heritage as well as that of regional Virginia. Monticello's continuing restoration signals a return to the Jeffersonian ideals of authenticity, self-sufficiency and hands-on food production—with the occasional indulgence. The impression of dedication, hard work and enjoyment of gardening and eating given by Thomas Jefferson's notes and letters is a clear predecessor to the work of Peter Hatch and Gabriele Rausse, as well as the work of the CHP. The enthusiasm, if not mania, Jefferson possessed for seed discovery and seed sharing makes it easy to imagine him strolling the setup at the Heritage Harvest Festival, listening thoughtfully to Joel Salatin or relishing homegrown heirloom tomato samples. Based on his love both for European-style wines and the beauty of nature, Jefferson could have easily been a mainstay at the Center for Historic Plants Wine & Roses events, drinking Gabriele Rausse's successful grapes under a soft June twilight. Visitors to Monticello can picture him working in the garden, planting strawberries and sampling figs as easily as they can watch their next-door neighbor garden, thanks to the reconstructive efforts of the Thomas Jefferson Foundation and the Monticello staff.

Perhaps it's so easy to imagine Jefferson participating in a variety of modern organizations and events because the area has maintained his spirit of enjoyment in and curiosity about the natural world. The more advanced the restoration of Monticello's horticultural beginnings becomes, the more obvious the connections between Jefferson's personal culinary enjoyments and those of modern Charlottesville. Jefferson's adages of manure compost, microclimes and seasonality have increasing relevance for individuals seeking an out from mass-produced, genetically modified food products purchased from cavernous warehouse stores. His insistence on quality and a do-it-yourself mentality can be seen in everyone from local restaurateurs turned homesteaders to young farmers popping up around the region. A Jeffersonian focus on the connections between good food with good beginnings and good health has not gone unnoticed by Charlottesville's farmers, gardeners and food producers.

Chapter 2

Outstanding in Their Field

Farming's New Wave

The Virginia Farm and Farmer Profile

The abundant fertility, long growing season and workable terrain of the Charlottesville area and its surrounding counties has not changed much since Jefferson's wildflower days in Shadwell. The kale in local garden beds still sprouts up with thick-leafed aplomb every spring through fall, and olives remain a bad fit for the climate and soil. The rhythmic seasons of planting and harvesting are still relevant markers of time in central Virginia. Intrepid pick-your-own-fruit enthusiasts can go to Carter Mountain in June for fresh peach ice cream or nectarines by the pound; they return in November for still-warm apple pies and a mountaintop full of Albemarle Pippins and Winesap apples. Hot summers aid the growth of heirloom tomatoes and watermelons, whether grown in the backyard or by one of the area's certified organic farmers. The seasons, landscape and soil of central Virginia provide the necessary foundation on which local farmers, growers and food producers can build businesses and feed residents.

According to the Virginia Department of Agriculture and Consumer Services (VDACS), agriculture is the largest industry in Virginia by a considerable margin. Agriculture provides the commonwealth with over $52 billion annually and employs over 300,000 Virginians.[47] The Virginia Farm Profile gives both a comprehensive and intimate representation of the kinds of farms—and farmers—in our state. On average, Virginia farmers are fifty-eight years old, with 30 percent of farmers clocking in at over sixty-five.[48] These workers own and operate over forty-six thousand individual farms, 90 percent of which are owned by individuals or families rather than major corporations.[49] Farms cover over one-third of our state's land area, amassing a total of 7.9 million acres.[50] By these numbers, every citizen in Charlottesville could own a farm of 100,000 acres, an area twenty times the size of Thomas Jefferson's original holdings in the region.

Both the farms and farmers of the Charlottesville MSA reflect statewide statistics and local color. As a geographic area, there are limitations to the types of sustenance that the state can produce. Virginia is not known as a grain state, nor have citrus or coffee ever been successfully mass-produced in our area. Sugar cane, rice, cocoa beans, spices and salt may be processed and repackaged in Virginia but are not produced in-state. South Street Brewery and Starr Hill may brew up delicious local beers, but the hops they use are mostly imported. Until recent years, producers of dairy, artisan meats and beef were hard to find in the commonwealth. The state's varied terrain, mild-yet-not-mild-enough weather and humidity prevent Virginia growers from producing many of the food options available in the Midwest or on the West Coast.

However, the list of what the state and central Virginia *can* grow and produce far outnumbers the list of "can nots." Discounting scores of mountain trout, seafood in Charlottesville comes from the eastern part of the state and provides a crucial element of Virginia's agricultural production. Aquaculture sales in the state exceed $30 million, with Chesapeake Bay– and Atlantic Ocean–caught fresh seafood appearing on plates from Virginia Beach to Winchester.[51] Succulent oysters jarred in brine are sold in gas stations along the Rockfish Valley Highway in Afton, culled from the Rappahannock River in the Northern Neck. Blue crabs, flounder and mahi-mahi pulled from the Atlantic and its tributaries nourish both the economy and Virginia diners. Though not exactly twenty-five-mile local, the Virginia aquaculture industry and its economic success serves all citizens of the state and the fine dining hotspots in Charlottesville as well.

Charlottesville-Albemarle's humid sub-tropical climate, with its frequent precipitation and long growing season, acts as a solid foundation for a variety of crops and agricultural products. From balmy April to brisk November, the multitude of options at the City Market on Saturday rivals that of San Francisco's Ferry Plaza or New York City's Union Square. Herb-coated goat cheese, smoked jowl bacon, fig jam, fresh blueberries, whole duck, green-purple field greens, elderflower cordial, corn tortillas and Ezekiel bread are just a fraction of the offerings available from various producers during the different seasons in the area. Farmers' markets in Charlottesville stretch from April to November, though local produce in the form of root vegetables and hardy winter greens can still be unearthed throughout the coldest months. The colors, textures, smells and tastes of local bounty far exceed what one would expect from a region divided by mountains, harnessed by wet summers and marked by high land prices.

Exactly how much farming takes place in the immediate locale of central Virginia? There are no fewer than twenty-five operational farms in the Charlottesville MSA, some of which fit the VDACS profile and many of which don't. Agriculture in central Virginia is a mix of trends and tradition, a mixture of heritage farmers and homesteaders. For every third-generation large-scale farmer, there seems to be an increasing number of smaller operations run by young families interested in wholesome food production. Many of Jefferson's interests in agriculture and horticulture, whether it be his general health-consciousness or desire for local economic solidarity, still factor into the reasons why farmers choose to either enter or stay in the agricultural sector.

For many, the business of farming is as much a career path as a lifestyle choice. The sheer number of hours that farm management requires, not to mention the attempted cooperation with nature and the threats to one's livelihood from circumstances outside of human control, prevents farming from being an easily compartmentalized, low-stress job. Battles with wildlife, land leases, government regulations, poor harvests, broken machinery and finicky customers are merely a handful of the challenges facing modern farmers, many of which are no different than the agricultural problems of Jefferson's time. Vacations for farmers are spare and hard earned, as are sick days or time off. The mountains that so mark the local landscape also create mudslides, road blockages and torrents of snow that can mark or mangle even the most well-run enterprise. To make order out of chaos in the form of a peach orchard, neat rows of peppers or pasture pens for chicken takes not only skill but also strong desire.

Agriculture in the Charlottesville-Albemarle area and its surrounding counties features a cast of characters as varied and flavorful as the crops themselves. There are the young guns, eager to put muscles and enthusiasm to work in place of experience and tradition. The homesteaders are a more ideological, perhaps Jeffersonian offshoot of the young farmers, a group whose interest in backyard pigs and fledgling apple orchards takes on the feel of anti-establishmentarianism. There are family operations both new and old, run by husbands and wives, three generations of men or an entire community. Some local producers have even become household names, showing up in the pages of *Southern Living* or on-screen in *Food, Inc.* Many of these farmers inhabit more than one of these roles, combining aspects of and interests in different trends and traditions. A feeling of camaraderie and inclusiveness makes such variety possible; there is a place for the newcomer in the stall right next to the inheritance farmer at the City Market every Saturday.

The agricultural underpinnings of the commonwealth's economy, coupled with its more than four hundred years of history, result in some long-term farming institutions. Virginia is home to 1,254 Century Farms, operations that have been maintained and family-run for over one hundred years.[52] The state government views family farming as a distinctly Virginian heritage, citing sustenance farming at Jamestown as foundational to our success as a state and a nation. Twenty-eight of these farms are located in the Charlottesville MSA, with nearby Augusta County boasting forty-six.[53] With the state government recognizing the importance of and achievements of heritage farming, it's no surprise that family-owned farms account for a majority of agricultural operations in Virginia. Yet it often doesn't take a century to establish a well-run farm that can be inherited by future generations.

Ownership of land is the most elemental necessity when preserving the family business, as many farmers have sold off their land to high-paying developers. Though the Virginia General Assembly initiated a farmland preservation effort in 2001, the offers of real estate and commercial developers can be all too alluring for farms not under VDACS's current one-thousand-acre area of protection.[54] If the land is there, dedication and interest are the next step toward establishing a generationally inherited enterprise. The willingness to continue in a farming parent's footsteps coincides with firsthand experience of the structure of an agriculturally focused household; before taking up the management of a dairy or an apple orchard, a son or daughter will have witnessed the physical, economic and social effects of a farming career choice on a parent. To continue a family investment in farming is no casual choice; it can be a calculated move to expand a business, a way of preserving property or simply a means of keeping family connections close and consistent.

Successful operations of inheritance farming often seem at ease with recent technological advances of the modern agricultural industry. Perhaps decades and generations of capitalizing on technological advancement and successful weathering of farming hardships have made modern family farms more receptive to using larger equipment and more corporate farming techniques. That's not to say that Virginia's Century Farms or well-established operations are corporatized and bloated. A familiarity with large-scale production methods and the need for a considerable workforce doesn't take the family out of the family farm; rather, successive generations have often proved essential in getting new technology and methods of production in place on aging operations.

Keeping Farms in the Family

A thriving community of many first-generation farms as well as lineage farms lies in the Shenandoah Valley in an area inhabited by Mennonites. These Mennonite farmers, often less visible to the Charlottesville food scene on account of conservative social practices and religious guidelines, have provided the area with large amounts of produce since establishing a community in Virginia in the eighteenth century.[55] Brett Wilson of Horse & Buggy Produce, a local grocery business, cites the Mennonite farmers as some of his major suppliers, responsible for the success of his business. Zach Miller of Timbercreek Organics in Charlottesville names Arlen Beery of Shenandoah Valley Family Farms Co-Op as a major influence on his farm's ethos due to Berry's "dedication to the best biological principles." In the case of the Mennonite farmers in the Shenandoah Valley, farming is as much a way of life as it a socio-religious occupation.

Outside of both Century Farms and community-wide long-term agricultural structures, family farms of a singular nature continue to act as the building blocks of Virginia agriculture. Donnie Montgomery of Homestead Creamery, an offshoot of his three-generations-old dairy farm in Franklin County, has carved out a niche of delectable, minimally processed dairy products. Running a business capable of selling ice cream in North Carolina and delivering fresh milk to local residents, Montgomery has been able to develop an inherited farm into an interstate business. He notes that a farm must develop and adjust like any business to the demands of the market and available resources. "I have to use more business tactics than I used to when we were smaller," Montgomery allows of his now-booming business. "The farm makes you a little more open-minded because you have to change and do things differently than you planned on doing."[56]

Such changes have occurred in the form of government aid, with Governor McDonnell funding the creamery with the first-ever grant from the Governor's Agriculture and Forestry Industries Development (AFID) in 2012.[57] Over a period of three years, this grant "will increase Homestead Creamery's purchases of Virginia-grown agriculture products by almost $1,500,000," as well as double its staff.[58] Montgomery seems most excited about this grant not for the additional revenue it will create but for the increased opportunity to reach more consumers. To Montgomery, the creamery looks forward to further growing the "traditional dairy methods that consumers are embracing as they seek all-natural products for their families."[59] The Virginia government is clearly interested in promoting these methods for both economic and health-conscious reasons.

An interest in protecting and providing for Virginia families underpins most of Montgomery's business ethos, whether it's keeping his own children involved in the farm and creamery or providing nutritious dairy for local families. At Homestead Creamery, grass-fed cows receive no antibiotics or growth hormones. The creamery's milk, contained in old-fashioned, thick glass bottles, has a list of all the additives that are *not* in the product. The creamery's silky, rich ice cream has no corn syrup and is based off a custard recipe so simple that Jefferson would have likely been able to produce it. Though the creamery produces over 500,000 gallons of milk a year, Homestead keeps family first in the midst of a large-scale production method.[60] According to Montgomery,

The Homestead Creamery milk truck. *Photo by Nancy Overton.*

the idea to turn his family's dairy business into a creamery stemmed from a desire to avoid a "mega-dairy" production; processing his own milk as well as the dairy of business partner David Bower allowed Montgomery and his two sons to add value to the farm's products and pay for the farm without converting to a larger format.

Families remain Donnie Montgomery's ideal—and actual—customer base, just as the business itself reflects his interest in preserving his inherited occupation. "I think some of the younger families have realized that they've gotten away from the farm long enough that their children don't understand how food is produced," Montgomery hypothesizes.[61] "I think it intrigues a lot of them that they can teach their children [about] that." The local food movement has provided considerable business for Homestead Creamery, as families interested in seeing exactly where their food comes from can take a trip to the facility for a day. The creamery's petting zoo, open house structure and welcoming country store create a wholesome, approachable experience that's attractive to people from six to sixty. Homestead Creamery's delivery business, a four-truck system that carries fresh, creamy milk to over one thousand families within an hour's drive, has an air of nostalgic Americana and promotes familial togetherness in its own way. Parents can spend less time grocery shopping and more at home with their kids, who are eager to drain the bottle and leave the empty glass out for the milkman to magically refill it the next morning or week.

To Montgomery, the allure of family business and family-based marketing is directly related to the benefit of community-forming: around dinner tables, or bowls of ice cream, people become connected and nourished. Montgomery notes the specific atmosphere of an ice cream shop as particularly dreamy, finding that "if you compared it to some businesses, usually when you come into an ice cream shop, you're coming in to relax or have fun." At Homestead Creamery, the concept of an ice cream social is still alive and relevant. One scoop of Lemon Crunch ice cream or a frozen take-home chicken potpie made from scratch with local chicken and eggs makes even the most worn-out urbanite feel comforted.

However, it doesn't require three generations' worth of practice to start and maintain a well-run family farming enterprise. Zach and Sara Miller of Timbercreek Organics have managed to create a thriving cattle, pig and poultry farm out of a former quarter horse training business. A drive to Timbercreek's meandering property on Garth Road in Charlottesville involves a good deal of free-roaming pigs, rolling green pastures and the tail-wagging of a couple farm dogs. Off the farm, Timbercreek has a much more luxe appeal. At Feast!, a local high-end grocery store, buyers can request translucent red slices of Timbercreek prosciutto, aged nearby at Kite's Hams in Wolftown, to pair with a variety of menus; rich, grass-fed beef from their farm appears around town everywhere from gourmet burger joints to high-class Italian restaurants. Yet for such a successful operation doing good business in a well-saturated market, the Millers appear to have started their farm on little more than excitement and curiosity.

When asked what experience or skill set with farming he possessed before starting Timbercreek, Zach Miller's enthusiastic response was, "None!" Armed with only a Joel Salatin book and a general interest in sustainability, Miller and his wife, Sara, started Timbercreek in 2007 as a fully integrated business. The integration comes in the form of carefully delineated and rotating spaces for cattle, poultry and pigs. Beef and poultry are linked through grazing and field prep, whereas the pigs use parts of the farm that don't fit perfectly in an evenly divided setting. The pigs rooting around in wired-in segments along the farm's driveway are as intentionally placed as the fields for cattle. A sense of harmony and closeness marks the Timbercreek operation as the kind of farm one dreams of nostalgically.

The concept of biomimicry is a crucial underpinning of the design of the farm's physical spaces as well as the choice in animals and plants to fill up those spaces. No animal species at Timbercreek can grow successfully without the others, based on the way the Millers cultivate their animals. Biomimicry "studies nature's best ideas and then imitates these designs and processes to solve human problems," according to biologist and sustainability consultant Janine Benyus.[62] Though this discipline has been applied to everything from the Coca-Cola Company to Colombian coffee farms, biomimicry has achieved headway on these several acres of prime Virginia farmland. The ecological interactions between landscape and animal species eliminate the need for pesticides, herbicides, fertilizers or antibiotics. Miller says their cattle provide the farm's most successful product, as the grass-fed and finished beef serves valuable ecological functions on the farm.

The Millers and the success of Timbercreek Farm are a variance on a current widespread trend in farming: the advent of the young farmer. As a response to the mechanization of farming practices that occurred in the 1970s, many new farmers are primarily interested in alternate forms of agricultural processes. Those who are just entering the agriculture industry—rather than growing up in it—often fall into the "young farmer" bracket of forty-and-under. Young to middle age, relative inexperience and general enthusiasm underpin their study and utilization of almost radically traditional methods of animal husbandry and horticulture on their operations. This particular bracket of newcomers includes both young adult farmers and those who have chosen agriculture after different career paths proved unsatisfying. Drawing inspiration from sources as varied as Joel Salatin's individualistic sustainability to medieval modes of efficiency, these young farmers, referred to as "greenhorns," often start with big ideas and little capital. Acquiring land is a challenge, as is learning the ropes of an industry before the wildlife roots out the succulent pleasures of pasture-penned chickens. The young farmers who are able to combine hard work and good fortune with quickly adaptable methods have fast become heavy-hitters in the local agriculture scene.

Greenhorns: Young Farmers at Work

To the Millers as well as many other young farmers, a business in agriculture offers both a career and a lifestyle choice. Often, the decision to farm for a living involves a rejection of a more corporatized American job structure with set hours and a predictable schedule, albeit with paid vacations. To Zach Miller, "you can have a lucrative profession or you can have a job that comes with a type of lifestyle that you don't have any reason to want to leave." In order to make Timbercreek an institution, the Millers understand the necessity of being physically rooted to their farm and land. Like the Century Farms before them or third-generation farmer Donnie Montgomery, the Millers view farming as a family operation and value it, in part, for this reason. A visit to Timbercreek Organics often means interacting with the Millers' toddlers, whose presence on the farm is as much a given as the Millers themselves. Zach states with pride that Timbercreek "is a family project." He acknowledges that "it has to be a viable business for us to survive" but notes that "we also recognize the importance of lifestyle it creates for us."[63]

The farming lifestyle, with its natural-seeming promotion of close bonding among individuals as well as between individuals and the land, has drawn more than locals to make a home and a business on a Virginia farm. Oklahoma-raised Erica Hellen, another young farmer who runs Free Union Grass Farm with her fiancé, Joel Slezak, settled into Free Union, Virginia, via an internship at Joel Salatin's monolith of an operation, Polyface Farms. In her late twenties with a laid-back attitude and a nose stud, Hellen looks more like a California surfer than a poultry and cattle farmer from Tulsa. If the close-knit family unit of the Millers offers one case study of young farmers, Hellen and her partner's nonchalant ease and cool-kid vibe lend an entirely unexpected face to another side of agriculture in Virginia.

Free Union Grass Farm is a patchwork operation, knitted together of various properties and various agricultural products into a useful, cohesive whole. Slezak and Hellen raise poultry and cattle, but what truly sets their farm apart is their sustainably raised and processed duck. Though many local farms offer pastured chicken, Hellen found that duck promised to be "the attention-getter that we needed" at their fledgling business. Though thick feathers and a watertight design make ducks harder to process, the lucrativeness of the waterfowl has allowed Hellen and Slezak to save money in other areas. A visit to the Free Union Grass Farms stall at the farmers' market offers one a taste of silky chicken liver pâté or the opportunity to take home some rendered duck fat, perfect for roasting potatoes.

While Joel Salatin's teachings on sustainability led Hellen, like Zach Miller, to agriculture, it is a love of the farming mindset that has kept her here. "It's not just a job," Hellen insists. "It's not a hobby—there's a tax bracket for those people." To Hellen and Slezak, farming is their "everything," both a reason to get going in the morning and the cause of many sleepless nights. "You can never just forget about it or put it away," Hellen states. "It's important to have the stress, you have to jive with that responsibility."[64] Though coyotes howling at night may keep Hellen and Slezak awake, the devotion Free Union Grass Farm's products have inspired in local restaurants and cooks has made Hellen and Slezak's hard-earned vacation and downtime that much sweeter.

The particular layout and geographic challenges of Free Union Grass Farm are reflective of a widespread issue for start-up farmers: high cost and low accessibility of farmable land. High land prices in Albemarle County offer a hurdle for young farmers to jump over before even getting to the growing stage.[65] Hellen and Slezak's operation has used no fewer than four different fields and properties since beginning in 2010. The farm now uses three different fields for raising its animals, operating on a total acreage of forty to fifty acres. Hellen notes, "It's tough in this particular part of the county to access affordable land in large quantities because it's either already owned by someone who's had it in their family forever or it's enormously expensive, or it's owned by some absentee landowner who doesn't really want anyone to use it, or it's in conservation and there are too many stipulations."

According to Tom Stanley of Virginia Cooperative Extension, "Rented farmland is essential to virtually every full-time farming operation and many part-time Virginia farmers."[66] Even if a farmer finds a landowner willing to lease their land, the actuality of what farming looks like can deter even the most well-intentioned landlord. Hellen has experienced firsthand the disconnect between what a landowner thinks a farm will look like and its physical mapping onto the landscape. "A lot of people in the community who want a happy, sustainable, organic Polyface-style farm also still want it to look like a golf course," Hellen admits. "That doesn't really always jive."

So what does an organically grown, sustainable farm look like? For Slezak and Hellen, it's a carefully orchestrated collection of parts and pieces made usable only through trial and error. In order to succeed as a start-up farm against such odds, a business has to be creative with its land use. In the case of Free Union Grass Farm, the result is a patchy network of different fields separated by roads and property lines. Like Timbercreek, Hellen and Slezak's operation relies heavily on rotation, both out of necessity and ideology. Hellen finds that the topographic layout of the property makes some areas better suited for cattle, others for chickens. Rotation at Free Union Grass Farm looks like daily movement of cows and chickens every two to four days. She laughingly tells a story of school buses waiting for Hellen and Slezak to herd cows across the road from one part of the farm to the next. She acknowledges, "It's all dependent on various factors, but every animal feeds every part of the farm at some point during the year."

Whether it's crop rotation, biomimicry or permaculture, young farmers like the Millers or Joel Slezak and Erica Hellen rely more on ideologies rather than physical accessories. There's no mention of pesticides, hormones, paid workers or other common topics that pertain to modern industrialized farming when talking to these farmers. While pasture pens take work to build, as does raising and processing ducks or cattle, these start-up farmers seem content, if not glad, to do the work themselves, relying on a spare hand or two lent by interns or visiting family. Books seem to be a major resource, as both farms rattle off several titles that have immensely helped their operation. These are small farms, capable of being run by two or three hardworking individuals whose excitement and interest help overcome hardships, long hours and insecure pacts with local wildlife.

Yet there are operations even more compact than Timbercreek Organics or Free Union Grass Farm, farms that still impact and shape the agricultural landscape of central Virginia in integral ways. An even smaller variety of small farmers, homesteaders have begun to appear with more frequency in and around Charlottesville and Albermarle, sometimes right in the backyard of downtown houses. These operations are often family-focused as well and perhaps even more ideologically motivated than other small farms. The goal of the homesteader is to produce wholesome food in a small-scale manner,

Joel Slezak and Erica Hellen. *Photo by Kevin Haney.*

seeking to avoid the chemicals and corporate overtones of big box stores. Zach Miller finds that part of the community appeal of Timbercreek lies in its adaptability to an even smaller scale of production. Zach notes, "There's been lately interest in homesteaders...our techniques can be scaled down to a couple acres." Whether it's a couple acres or several yards in one's backyard, homesteading has become a viable option for those interested in creating an alternate food lifestyle without depending on agriculture for their livelihood.

HOMESTEADING AND THE SELF-SUSTAINING ENTERPRISE

Homesteading as a lifestyle choice and economic choice of going back to the land, so to speak, has existed since Roman times. The story of Cincinnatus, who forsakes political glory and worldly riches for his small farm, is not dissimilar from the retreat of George Washington back into Mount Vernon's verdant arms in 1797. Homesteading, as defined by author in self-sufficiency John Seymour, is the decision to "live independently in harmony with the land."[67] Certain skills are required of the self-sufficient homesteader, including the "harnessing [of] natural forms of energy, raising crops and keeping livestock, preserving foodstuffs, making beer and wine, basketry, carpentry, weaving," among other skills.[68]

Urban homesteaders grow edible gardens on rooftops in Brooklyn, while more agrarian homesteaders often revamp acres of property into models of land-mindfulness. Charlottesville offers prime real estate for homesteaders via two channels: fertile, workable land and an inquisitive, intellectual environment. Even from the earliest days of Jeffersonian self-sufficiency and the university's founding, the area has been populated with freethinking individuals interested in the connection between food and lifestyle. Charlottesville's locus as an artistically minded and liberal community filled with political refugees, resident artists and activists acts as foundational to the success of homesteading ventures in the area. While farmhouses in Scottsville or big yards on Northwood Avenue may give homesteaders the physical underpinnings of their venture, the can-do mentality promoted by the university and Charlottesville citizens helps give these ideas flight.

Will Richey of the restaurants Revolutionary Soup and the Whiskey Jar is a prime example of a successful modern-day homesteader. Richey; his wife, Lisa; and their two children live in an old blue farmhouse with a tin roof out in Esmont, a twenty-minute drive from downtown Charlottesville. Their two-acre property is studded with fledgling apple trees whose early fruit has been plucked to promote root growth and carefully selected indigenous plants. Friendly pigs squeal around in their pasture pen, while ducks and chickens stake out another edge of the yard. A good-sized pond, bordered by pawpaw trees and wineberry bushes, lies next to a large garden plot chock-filled with tomato vines and asparagus plants grown wild, their long, yarrow-like fronts tickling bare legs. Richey even looks the part of an old-time farmer, with suspenders, a beard and a large gap-toothed grin.

Richey's foundation for homesteading lies with his English degree from the University of Virginia instead of a farming internship or family heritage. Ruskin and Morris are major influences, with their founding of the Arts and Crafts movement and their appreciation of a minimalist medieval aesthetic. Ruskin, Morris and Richey value craftsmanship and doing things by hand in an honest and humble manner—"work for work's sake and craftsmanship for craftsmanship's sake," as Richey titles it. John Seymour's book *The Self-Sustaining Life and How to Live It* proved invaluable when Richey and his wife actually began structuring their new life and new farm, as "the title itself was what we were looking for: we wanted a self-sustaining life." The pigs Richey raises go toward feeding both his household and the Whiskey Jar; in several years, he hopes to make his own cider and currently produces enough fruit and vegetables in their garden to provide for the family and a couple farmhands passing through.

When asked what motivated he and Lisa's decision to become homesteaders, Richey simply summarizes his new lifestyle as stemming from "Generation X anti-establishmentarianism." Early on, Richey rebelled against the Northern Virginia suburban mindset. The beauty of a homesteading lifestyle to the Richeys is that it offers the family "a whole life." "I'm growing the food that I eat," Richey notes. "I'm providing for my family. We don't have the typical farmhouse—the land has to look nice, too, we have to do it in an aesthetically pleasing way, and permaculture works with that." Permaculture, to the Richeys, is an aspect of "everything working together."

Permaculture factors greatly into the concept of homesteading at Red Row Farm, as well as the operations of Timbercreek Organics and Free Union Grass Farm. As much a design discipline as an agricultural practice, permaculture has becoming an integral part of the face of modern sustainability. The term itself, an integration of *permanent* and *agriculture*, "is an integrated design philosophy that encompasses gardening, architecture, horticulture, ecology, even money management and community design."[69] Waste recycling and the creation of systems that meet their own needs are also basic tenets of permaculture.[70] Bill Mollison, launcher of the permaculture movement, also cites "care of the earth," "care of the people" and "return of surplus" as foundational principles of the design. The daily rotation of cattle at Free Union Grass Farm, the placement of various animal species at different points along the Millers' property and the careful pairing of apple trees with indigenous vegetation at Red Row Farm are all examples of local farmers and thinkers melding thought with practice into sustainable landscapes.

The Many Faces—and Founders—of Sustainable Agriculture

Terms like permaculture, organic, sustainable and green have become buzzwords in the modern food industry. They act as rallying cries for new farmers eager to provide healthier alternatives to the products of industrial farming. They offer a recognizable code by which consumers can recognize and differentiate grocery products. These words, however, are relatively recent additions to mainstream discussions of food and food practices.

Joel Salatin at Polyface Farms. *Photo by Jessica Reeder.*

Documentaries like *Food, Inc.* and *Supersize Me*, the vegetarian meanderings of Mark Bittman and food-related news reportage and the success of Michael Pollan's existentially inquisitive *In Defense of Food* have brought issues of sustainable and organic agriculture to the wider American consciousness. Media such as these examples cause us to rethink those lunchtime fast-food splurges or find an alternate to the corporatized and trademarked chicken breasts on sale at big box stores lining the roads. Yet the roots of this movement lie not with the *New York Times* or graduate school classrooms but with the anti-establishmentarian interests of contrarian farmers and thinkers, particularly one straw hat–wearing Virginia native named Joel Salatin.

Joel Salatin and Polyface Farms are almost as recognizable figures as Earthbound Organics or Horizon Dairy. Sustainably raised, pasture-penned Polyface chickens end up roasted in Charlottesville, fried up in Richmond or stewed in Washington, D.C. The farm offers an incredible variety of products, selling eggs, pork, beef, turkeys, rabbits and even lumber to a group of people so devoted that they drive 150 miles for meat.[71] The man who famously refused to ship Michael Pollan a steak runs a farm to which he refers as "beyond organic," a food so clean that a USDA Organic label doesn't begin to capture the quality of its products.[72] Interviewed by the *New York Times* and immortalized on camera in *Food, Inc.* and *Fresh*, Salatin, as a self-described "Christian-libertarian-environmentalist-capitalist-lunatic-Farmer," offers one of the more colorful—and recognizable—figures of modern sustainable agriculture.

Salatin is a second-generation farmer at Polyface, a child of parents who bought the farm in 1961 with the hopes of "healing" the damaged, nutrient-depleted property in the Shenandoah Valley.[73] Innovations such as tree-planting for soil protection, pasture pens, "multispecies grazing rotations," a mobile chicken coop and composting seem like givens today in modern sustainable agricultural outputs but proved positively revolutionary in an age of Nixonian food industrialization. To the workers and owners of Polyface, the farm stands as "America's premier non-industrial food production oasis," owing part of its success to the belief that "the Creator's design is still the best pattern for the biological world."[74]

Even for an operation the size of Polyface, with its processing of twelve thousand broiler chickens yearly, family values remain a crucial foundation for the farm. Salatin relates, "From my earliest memories, I loved the farm."[75] Whether influenced by his grandfather's octagonal chicken coop or his great-uncle's commercial chicken farm, Salatin allows that "some of [his] fondest childhood memories are of seeing…thousands of chickens out on the field."[76] Marked by the same "farming bug" that captured his father, an "incredible innovator," Salatin has succeeded in creating a business and lifestyle that has been inherited by his own children and, ideally, by theirs as well.[77] The author of books such as *Family Friendly Farming*, Salatin views farming as a family venture made to support a group of people genetically tied as well as ideologically connected. Salatin treats his farm as a pulpit, educating consumers on the values of sustainable agriculture as well as the importance of family and an environmentally conscious lifestyle. The innovations and ideas of this particular "lunatic farmer" have shaped the agricultural future of both central Virginia and the United States in inescapable ways; the work of Polyface has excited, energized, confounded and challenged young farmers who intern for Salatin or pick up a copy of one of his many books. Though Erica Hellen may adapt Salatin's pasture pens for her own farm, the foundation of a Polyface-bred sustainable sensibility has proven as invaluable to agriculture in the Charlottesville area as Jefferson's original experiments with vinoculture and English peas.

The intrepid, do-it-yourself spirit of Jefferson, Salatin and countless other farmers in central Virginia appears with a vengeance in Gail Hobbs-Page's Caromont Farm. Her operation, which produced 125,000 pounds of goat's milk and cow's milk cheese in 2012, reflects a Jeffersonian interest in making the down-home into the gourmet. Hobbs-Page started in 2007 with 3,000 pounds of milk in a young upstart dairy; a former head chef at several Charlottesville fine-dining hotspots, she was looking for an opportunity to be in the food industry without having to cook. Influenced by a French cheesemonger in Charlottesville, Hobbs-Page purchased twenty-five acres in Esmont and dairy goats while still cooking professionally, keeping a "goat diary" to keep track of her findings.

In the past six years, Caromont Farm has almost single-handedly developed the cheesemaking industry in Virginia. With fresh chevre sold at Murray's Cheese in New York City and various cheeses making it onto the menu at Sean Brock's restaurant Husk in Charleston, Caromont has

Gail Hobbs-Page with her farm dogs. *Photo by Casey Ireland.*

become a household name for luxurious and reasonably priced American artisanal cheese. But Hobbs-Page attributes her success less to Jefferson's food heritage and more to the consumers of Charlottesville. "It's the people, really," Hobbs-Page insists. "I don't think you can put this on Jefferson. We had a pig slaughter here on Saturday, and I looked around and there were four butchers, two winemakers, four photographers, six chefs, and I thought, 'Where else would that happen?'"[78] Her joy in belonging to the community is matched only by her solid reputation as a no-nonsense, dependable producer of quality products accessible to a variety of consumers with a variety of tastes. The influence of European cheesemaking, combined with a personal southern heritage and hands-on experience with fine dining, makes Caromont Farm and Gail Hobbs-Page one of the most distinctly Charlottesvillian agricultural producers in the area.

Whether young or old, transplants or natives, farmers in the Charlottesville MSA have maintained a tradition of Virginia agricultural excellence that began with Jefferson's own horticultural dabbling. Both the quality of the land and the intellectual fertility of the city itself have created a hospitable climate for modern—and old-fashioned—farms. The area has been host to a variety of national and localized trends, whether the prolonged success of the family farm or the old-is-new allure of homesteading. Chickens, pigs and cattle grow more naturally, enhance the landscape more fully and just plain taste better under a free-ranging plan guided by permaculture and sustainability. Connecting farming as an occupation with family life has been a major concern for local farmers, whether they are just starting out or have incorporated business and family for generations. Inquiring, developing, advancing and innovating are the marks of a central Virginia farmer, one who chooses agriculture as both a career and a lifestyle.

A notion of food as inspiring togetherness, whether at the table, in the community or within the family, starts on the farm before it gets to the kitchen. Marbled cuts of beef, crisp greens, plump figs and ripe cheeses offer meals in themselves and exude flavors that represent seasons, terroir and the hands of an individual. Before an ingredient gets to the City Market or grocery store, a farmer has planted, raised, grown or tended it with both practicality and ideology. Given that a cook is only as good as his ingredients and a gourmet store is only as luxurious as its products, the farm has proven to be a crucial first step in forming a regional culinary heritage. The variety, quality and uniqueness of Virginia's agricultural output is only matched by the treatment these products get by restaurateurs and retailers.

Chapter 3

Food Hubs

Getting Regional Ingredients to the Home Cook

The Locavores of Charlottesville

After Timbercreek Organics has cured its salty-sweet prosciutto at Kite's and Gail Hobbs-Page has finished packaging a creamy round of Bloomsbury cheese, an extra step is needed before the home cook can transform these ingredients into something magical. Even if the farmers or producers themselves sell their own products, such direct marketing to the customer requires them to put on a new hat: that of the retailer. From vegetable stands in parking lots on Preston Avenue to the endless treasure-trove of local international grocer Foods of All Nations, consumers can purchase a variety of different Charlottesville food products at a variety of price points from retail settings as unique as they are delightful.

At every stall of locally produced goods at the City Market and behind the glass at cheese counters, butchers and wine stores resides an expert—or at least someone with a good story to tell about a product. The clerk at the Organic Butcher may tell you how to cook a challenging cut of pork, while another at Mona Lisa Pasta offers suggestions for a sauce to top hand-cut squid ink pappardelle. People in Charlottesville may shop at Whole Foods, Harris Teeter and Kroger to get necessities, but it is the locally owned and run grocery retailers who earn the most committed following. These shops appeal to Charlottesville's love of community; they provide the old-fashioned pleasure of walking into a shop and being recognized by name. It's an offering of a particularly juicy plum, a sample of cheese or an after-

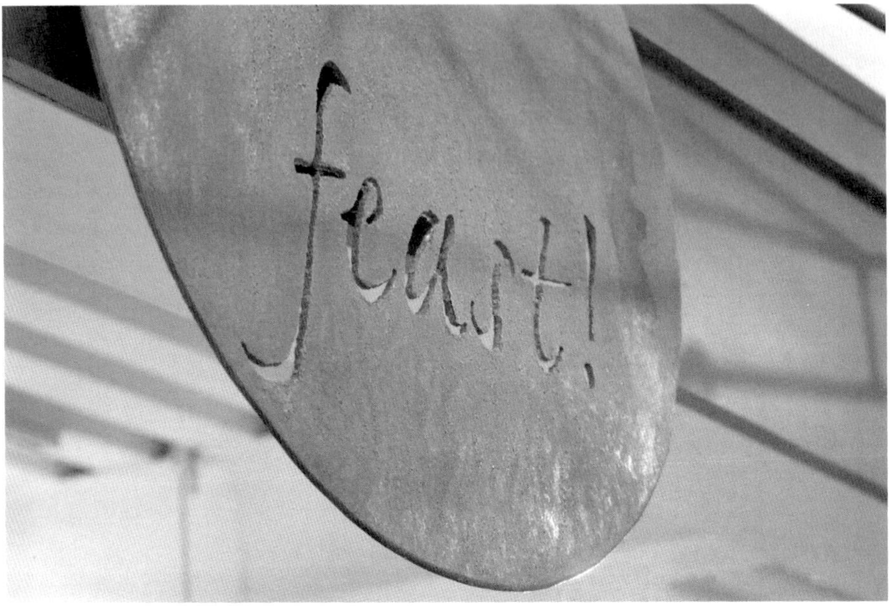

The eponymous sign at Feast! *Photo by Kevin Haney.*

hours wine tasting that makes Charlottesville's food retailers so successful and so well loved.

An understanding of the market for local goods in Charlottesville naturally precedes a discussion of the various kinds of retailers from whom customers can purchase these goods. The wealth of some of Charlottesville and Albemarle County's citizens is locally understood and nationally acknowledged, with *Forbes* magazine listing Charlottesville's wealthiest as the thirteenth most prosperous group in the nation.[79] With an average of 5.2 percent of this income set aside for charity, it's clear that there's a sizable contingent of individuals and families with a considerable disposable income and various ways to spend it. The music venues, theaters, arts community and restaurant scene are incredibly vibrant in central Virginia, drawing in both tourists and those hoping to create a home in the midst of mountaintop views and high culture. The University of Virginia and its teaching hospital draw in doctors, professors and highly educated individuals who are well versed in current affairs at both a culinary and a global level.

Perhaps it's no surprise then, given the trend toward organic, sustainable agriculture that has occurred within the last decade, that a community aided by the wealthy, enlightened by the educated and charmed with a southern appreciation of good meals and good fun has an abundance of citizens who deeply care about their food. To eat locally and sustainably, despite the war cry of traditional, back-to-our-roots marketing, is often to eat expensively. Which is not to say that there aren't plenty of affordable options for lower-income families hoping to eat local or individuals seeking to make these options more accessible. Stephanie Andregg-Maloy of the City Market works closely with Charlottesville organizations for the elderly and the underprivileged youth to make market goods available to people

A monthly selection of *Edible Blue Ridge*. *Photo by Kevin Haney.*

from all walks of life. Similarly, it's possible to shop at a gourmet grocery store like Feast! and get healthy local food for under ten dollars, thanks to the smaller packaging of produce and products. According to several farmers and producers in Charlottesville, local, organic foodstuffs can be accessible to a variety of incomes with budget adjustments. However, a large portion of the audience purchasing free-range duck, farm eggs and homemade Boursin cheese appears to have a larger budget to adjust.

In 2006, Meg McEvoy, a journalist for popular newspaper *C-VILLE Weekly*, wrote an article titled simply "The $5 Tomato." In this article, McEvoy discusses in no uncertain terms "a certain kind of Charlottesvillian" who "moves through the small sections of imported crackers and little jars of tangy tapenade…hunting for food in her native habitat" in the hallowed aisles of Feast![80] This woman picks up an heirloom tomato, weighs it and takes it, with satisfaction, to the register, where it rings up for $5. Even in 2006, McEvoy notes that "this rarified world of high-end organic and artisanal foods has exploded locally"—even more crucially, she finds that "to truly understand the trend, you've got to leave the market, get back in the SUV, and head out of town."[81]

The paradoxical economics of paying more for an unsophisticated, lumpy, hundred-year-old variety of tomato have been capitalized even further in other parts of the country. In 2010, Sotheby's Auction House in New York City held an auction for crates of heirloom vegetables drawn from nearby farms and growers. The starting price per box? A mere $1,000. The benefit auction, titled "The Art of Farming," was a first for Sotheby's and took place in the Manhattan showroom of the auction house.[82] The contrast between heirloom pumpkins and a world-renowned auction house is a startling one, just as the $5 price of a single tomato seems a surprising food choice, if not an exorbitant one.

What Sotheby's and the "certain kind of Charlottesvillian" understand about these high-priced, old-fashioned varieties of produce, a knowledge all too limited to those with disposable income or a higher level of education, is the economics of taste. The citrusy tartness of a Green Zebra tomato, the rich smoothness of a heritage pumpkin and the surprise beauty of fresh-picked carrots, with their smell of Queen Anne's lace and knobby irregularities, are treasures of memory and the taste buds. The thought of a relished childhood BLT is most closely invoked by the smell of a homegrown beefsteak rather than a hothouse, imported hybrid. The remembrance of a great-aunt's strawberry preserves is replicated more easily in a jar bought at a roadside stand than on the sugar-free aisle of a nearby super-saver.

The connection between food and memory, between farmer and customer, between the land and the bounty it provides is an all-powerful tie all too distant from modern consumerist patterns. What people in Charlottesville understand in regard to the food they get and the places they get it from is the complex, unadulterated pleasure of buying local products and the economic satisfaction it brings to the individual and the community.

The Gourmet Grocer

Grocery stores abound in the Charlottesville-Albemarle area, both individually owned and big-box. Gas stations in disguise offer handcrafted cappuccinos along with a tank of regular, while larger, more traditional-seeming operations offer bouquets of local tulips along with cans of Folgers. No matter what size or company, all grocery stores in the area know to cater to the epicurean interests of many of Charlottesville's citizens. The gourmet store, a popular sight in the area, caters to the tastes of discerning palates even more directly, whether proudly marketed and displayed on Main Street or tucked away off the Rockfish Gap Highway en route to Crozet. While it may be difficult to purchase boxes of dishwasher detergent or bags of dog food in these shops, those looking for cheeses, wines, local produce and a variety of artisanal products find their needs well met.

These gourmet stores are perhaps the most local of them all, run by Charlottesville natives or happy transplants with stories, smiles and never-ending culinary knowledge. This is the place where one is most likely to find the freshest herbs, most interesting *salame* or best dried pasta outside of the farmers' markets. Particular markets have cult followings, whether it's the die-hard dolma lover who picks up two dozen from Mona Lisa Pasta each week or the Crane Crest Real French Dressing fanatic who purchases two cases every holiday season from Feast! at the Main Street Market. Gourmet markets offer customers two commodities: delicious ingredients and the share of knowledge on how to use them.

Feast!, the market and eatery of Kate Collier and Eric Gertner's creation, has become a staple of the Charlottesville gourmet scene since opening its doors in 2002. A vaguely industrial space, housed in the larger structure of the Main Street Market, Feast! has both a welcoming and a utilitarian feeling. The uncluttered layout of the store, with its deli and cheese counters, dry goods section, wine rack and produce stand, facilitates easy browsing—

The lunch cafe at Feast! *Photo by Kevin Haney.*

and easy tasting. Samples of everything from duck liver pâté to house-made pimento cheese dot the entire store. When visiting, a shopper can almost make a meal out of the bits of cheese, spoonfuls of caramel and handfuls of nuts strategically placed in various sections. A walk-up café allows customers to try ingredients they wouldn't have otherwise been exposed to. Fresh sweet corn, slivers of extra-aged gouda or house-spiced nuts excite customers' taste buds and allow Feast! to showcase the best local ingredients in an accessible manner.

Offering the best of what the area produces and importing the best of what it can't has been a prime mission of Kate Collier since opening the store with her now-husband, Eric Gertner. The daughter of a Fauquier County culinary entrepreneur who became famous thanks to horseshoe-shaped shortbread cookies, Collier has been a part of the Charlottesville food scene since a young age. "My brother and I were involved in that, from rolling out the dough and cutting the horseshoes to her dressing us up in riding outfits and sending us to Neiman Marcus to hand out samples," Collier says with a laugh.[83] After working among chefs in San Francisco and a brief sojourn in Europe, Collier returned to Virginia with the goal of creating documentary films about the communal aspects of food before seizing an opening at the Main Street Market and beginning her business.

Collier is another heir to Jefferson's high-low mix of gourmet and garden-variety. "It was mostly about cheese and perfectly sliced prosciutto and some local produce," Collier relates of Feast!'s beginnings. However, the beauty and bounty of local produce has been Collier's focus since day one. "We've always been 'local first' and telling the story of the local producers and offering samples," she relates. The samples, quite literally, put the experience of local eating right into a customer's mouth and negate the need for much preaching from Collier or any of her employees at Feast! To any customer who's tried a bite of Virginia ham off a toothpick or snacked on a swipe of fresh chevre on a cracker knows the power of Collier's methodology. However, Collier is quick to point out that a *good food* store is not necessarily a *health food* store. "We're not buying into every new trend," Collier insists, though gluten-free options have made headway at the store. "We're curating a collection of great food; we're not trying to offer them every option in the world."

So who are the customers taking advantage of this collection? Collier cites her market as a diverse one, noting that over half of her customers are women. "The common denominator is people that love good food and find value in buying and eating it," Collier says. Feast! draws customers of a certain taste with specific expectations as to the quality of products and their places of origin. Fresh arugula from a local farm cozies up to organic Hass avocados from Florida, while a round of Monastery Gouda from Crozet sits next to selections from Holland in the cheese case. It seems that Feast! shoppers expect the best of what central Virginia has to offer, whether it's produce or cured meats or horseshoe-shaped shortbread, without losing an interest in general gourmet niceties. Collier's desire to own a good foods store means that it's not incompatible to showcase both local fare and imported Parmesan and French wine.

Collier has found that her store attracts a lot of regulars, people who visit upward of four times a week for either lunch or groceries. Feast!'s central location, easily accessible by those downtown as well as the UVA hospital with commuters aided by a large parking area, allows for quick stop-ins and leisurely lunches. Though shoppers may get their San Pellegrino in bulk at Sam's Club, the easily customizable structure of Collier's store allows for buying in small quantities. "European-style marketing" is a popular option at Feast!, meaning that customers choose to do their shopping throughout the week rather than in a single fell swoop on a Sunday or weekday. Collier finds that Feast! works well for single people "because you can get smaller amounts than you can at big-box stores."

Collier's ownership of Feast! is not the only role she plays in the Charlottesville food scene. Along with co-founder Marisa Vrooman, Collier started a consolidating distribution nonprofit, Local Food Hub, in 2009. According to Collier, the "primary short-term goal is to develop events, educational programs and local connections to enable our community to be more involved in our local food system."[84] Ideally, the Local Food Hub, along with local food production, will "[contribute] to land ownership, [build] a stronger tax base, [create] opportunity for entrepreneurship in the areas of farm inputs and support services, and [encourage] responsible land stewardship for the future."[85]

The Local Food Hub works with Relay Foods, a popular online grocery retailer; numerous restaurants; and other food-related small businesses to funnel larger quantities of local produce into the local economy. Emily Manley of the Local Food Hub notes that the nonprofit provides small farmers with "the infrastructure and services they need to access schools, hospitals, grocery stores, and other markets that they have traditionally been unable to reach."[86] All these products, including "locally grown fruit, vegetables, meat, eggs, and value-added items from more than 70 small family farms in Central Virginia," are stored at a central warehouse with 3,500 square feet and multiple temperature zones. The Food Hub ships these products out to over 150 regional locations in an eighteen-foot refrigerated delivery truck and refrigerated van. For businesses unable to sample their way through Feast! or buy in bulk from the farmers' market, the Local Food Hub provides an essential path for funneling local ingredients into receptive channels.

As with the core structure of the Local Food Hub, which carries food from farmers "fresh, frozen, and preserved" through every month of the year, seasonal agriculture gives a backbone to Feast! The produce selection changes with the seasons, as do many of the samples and the café offerings. Collier describes the seasonality of Feast!'s offerings with poetic delight. "In winter, when kale and turnips and greens are plentiful, there's kale every day in soups, roasted turnips," she notes. "In the summertime, the menu drips with tomatoes and basil. Seasonality is what keeps Feast! really fresh." The café offers a seasonal special grilled cheese and a seasonal special salad, which allows Feast! to consistently buy from local farmers.

Whether through the Local Food Hub, Feast! or personal experience, Collier is a wealth of knowledge about local farmers and agriculture. Having formerly employed Joel Slezak of Free Union Grass Farm and responsible for the success of Cville Candy Company, Collier has an apparent eye for nurturing culinary talent. The trend of young farmers and homesteaders has not gone unnoticed, nor has the increased specialization of certain farms. Such specialization works for businesses like Feast!, which now have the opportunity to order from farmers with heritage products almost tailor-made for menus and fine dining.

Outside the Big Box: CSAs and Online Retailers

The success of the gourmet grocer in Charlottesville reflects one side of its unique culinary tastes: the taste for the fancy, the unique, the highbrow. Yet the down-home, get-your-hands-dirty and meet-your-farmer appeal of community-supported agriculture connects with an overlapping yet distinct interest of the area. Community-supported agriculture programs, or CSAs, abound in the area, subscribed to by a variety of customers. College students, young mothers and die-hard hippies can all go to the farm or to a pickup site to grab their "subscription": a basket of the freshest fruits and vegetables the farm can produce. A CSA's most basic purpose is to link the producer and consumer directly, allowing for a greater understanding of food origins and a deeper appreciation of local food sourcing.

CSA subscriptions can vary in subscription length, size and frequency of pickups. One of the constants of CSA-style grocery buying is the consistency of beautiful, just-picked vegetables, fruit, flowers and herbs. The relationship between farmer and consumer in this case is a symbiotic one: the CSA subscriber gets direct access to the freshest local produce, and farmers get funding upfront at the beginning of growing season. If bad weather, machinery problems or unforeseen issues disrupt the growing season or the farm's ability to produce, both farmer and subscriber shoulder the burden of costs. This alternative to more conventional, industrialized methods of food distribution gives the customer a more active role in food production and allows the farmer to keep his or her products locally purchased.

But what happens if a consumer wants to try different offerings from different farms? What if a long drive to the farm isn't part of one's getting-off-work schedule? Though the economic and agricultural model of community-supported agriculture is a thriving business in Charlottesville, others have figured out a way to promote the CSA culture with less time and more options. Brett Wilson of Horse & Buggy Produce has figured out a way to offer grocery subscriptions with a flexibility that fits a variety of lifestyles. Horse & Buggy allows customers to purchase weekly or biweekly shares of products such as produce, dairy, bread, dry goods and various meats. Shares are available for pickup or home delivery, a boon for those too busy to schedule time for meet-up sites.

With a well-tailored website and an easy personality, Brett Wilson has a Yale education and a love of heirloom tomatoes. Horse & Buggy began officially in 2006, unofficially in 2004, when Wilson was growing produce for restaurants and peddling cider. One day, a group of local women saw the produce in the back of Wilson's pickup truck and inquired about his foodstuffs. The demand for his product exceeded its supply, so Wilson partnered with Mennonite farmers in the valley. Due to such "mom requests," Wilson made his produce available in 2006 via Horse & Buggy subscriptions.

Wilson's partnership with the Mennonite farmers, born from the realization that his own farming capacity was not suitable for keeping up with the demand for heirloom products, is crucial to his business. Wilson himself is no longer a farmer but a distributor. Having to make the choice between roles and lifestyles, Wilson chose to "be the link between populations," whether the populations are grower and consumer or the Mennonite community and the local populace at large.[87] Wilson's decision to buy from the Mennonites led to an exodus from conventional jobs for the community members, who have now begun raising poultry and dairy as well as produce. Beaming, Wilson tells the story of a Mennonite man whom Wilson has seen grow from childhood, now the owner of a five-acre produce farm partially funded by Horse & Buggy.

Wilson is now considering adding organic, regional and conventional items to Horse & Buggy's traditionally local offerings, seeing as "people still eat bananas." "We can't be so absolute in our convictions that we ignore what people need," Wilson insists. Horse & Buggy itself is now a year-round operation, freezing berries, cider, cherries and tomatoes and offering black beans and non-produce foodstuffs such as Albemarle Baking Company bread and Aqui Es Mexico tortillas to round out its offerings.

Wilson's idea to combine the freshest of available local products with offerings more likely found at a supermarket chain has already been taken a step further by a company that has established a veritable online grocery empire in Virginia over the last several years. Online grocery stores are the kind of thing one sees advertised on the New York subway, a standby of larger cities where convenience is king and fresh produce can be hard to come by. Yet Zach Buckner, an electrical engineer from Lexington, has discovered a way to make a virtual headway into "the biggest business in the world" with his company, Relay Foods.[88]

Browsing Relay Foods' website is like walking through Whole Foods, the farmers' market and your neighborhood quick-mart all at once. One can buy No-Bull gourmet veggie burgers, AA batteries, Tropicana orange juice and quail eggs from Down Branch Farm with a click of a mouse. Relay offers an incredible selection of local produce, from red Russian kale to canary melons. Weekly Bounty Baskets, which change daily as well as seasonally, allow customers to pick up a CSA-style assortment of produce, albeit from different farms and at a no-commitment price. For those too nervous to commit to a subscription or too curious to stick to one farm, these Bounty Baskets have the excitement of a CSA bundle without the insecurity or the commitment.

But Relay's allure lies with its foothold in more markets than just the local food scene. Many Whole Foods products, including its often-organic and reasonably priced 365 brand, are available online for those craving quality ketchup without wanting to brave the traffic at Whole Foods' location on Hydraulic Road. Conversely, cheaper-priced food items like Richfood or similar off-brands are also available on Relay, thanks to a partnership with Reid Super-Save Market on Preston Avenue. Household cleaning products and cat litter line up with organic bell peppers and frozen pizzas from Mona Lisa Pasta on an easily navigable, user-friendly website that has made converts out of even the staunchest in-person market-goer. Similar to Horse & Buggy, Relay customers can have their groceries delivered to their home for a fee or can pick them up from a variety of centrally located stops in Charlottesville and Albemarle County five days out of the week.

Zach Buckner's design of the business belies his engineer roots. A self-proclaimed empiricist, Buckner's goal for the business is to be a one-stop shop for everything a big-box store could offer. A knowledge of freight costs, business efficiency and gas prices makes Relay not only convenient to customers but ultimately a more cost-effective option for both business and consumer. Though groceries are a trillion-dollar industry with an almost limitless customer base, Buckner admits that Relay customers are particularly well-educated people interested in food quality and origin. "It just so happens that the people who are quickest to understand what we're doing are people that have college degrees," Buckner states. Even Relay's more than forty-five employees have an unusually high level of education, matching their enthusiasm for business with individualized savviness that contributes to a tightknit team. College graduates with four languages under their belts have driven grocery trucks, while MBAs man the desks.

Though CSAs and gourmet grocery stores have a niche local appeal, Relay has its eyes on a larger piece of the grocery industry pie. With bases in Richmond, Charlottesville, Williamsburg, Baltimore and Washington, D.C., the company is the largest online food marketplace in the mid-Atlantic region.[89] Buckner's goal for the company is not an overblown monopoly; it's something far more idealistic. "I would love to see a Charlottesville that had no strip malls and no big-box stores," Buckner muses. He looks forward to creating "the day when good food is flowing to houses around Charlottesville at something more like that ten cents per ton per mile instead of that forty-five dollars per ton per mile." "The traffic in Charlottesville is decimated," he continues rhapsodically, "and there's farming and baking and making chocolate." It's not too challenging to imagine that his Pleasantville reverie could actually impact the landscape of the area, with more and more grocery items being listed every day that consumers can purchase in a more efficient, convenient matter.

Going to Market

Entrance to the Saturday City Market in downtown Charlottesville. *Photo by Kevin Haney.*

But convenience isn't the deciding factor in grocery store selection for many people who prefer a more communicative, collaborative market environment. The traditional marketplace image, filled with people, fragrances, noises and tastes, appears on a converted parking lot every Saturday from April to December. The farmers' market can be as simple as a couple vendors intermingling in a small space behind a college building or as large and complex as the four-day bonanza at Union Square Market. In Charlottesville, farmers' markets have been in full swing since at least 1972, when a man named George Cason ran for the Charlottesville City Council. His platform included a plan for a new, accessible farmers' market, "a place where the public could purchase locally grown foods sold by the growers themselves."[90] The city's assistant manager quickly latched onto Cason's concept, despite his defeat in the election, and soon began hatching a plan for the market's design.

Agriculture and food production was, for Cason as well as many others, a family affair from the beginning. "I've been in the produce business all my life—my daddy was too," Cason noted. In 1973, he and his three brothers began the market, initially the only vendors selling. Cason and two of his brothers still sell at the farmers' market, though a Cason nephew has been banned due to being overly "boisterous."[91] The City Market's current layout and status—a welcoming, exciting place for both locals and visitors—meets Cason's conception of the market. "I just knew it would turn out like this," Cason muses, "that it would be a nice place for people to come and meet each other and enjoy the morning."

People have been enjoying the morning at the City Market for over forty years now. It's a place to grab breakfast, whether a fresh-made omelet or piping-hot donuts with a side of Shenandoah Joe's coffee. It's a place to meet friends, whether you go with a gaggle of fellow UVA students or take the whole family, newborns included. It's a small business incubator; many local businesses that started out as a stall at the City Market now run good-sized and well-known operations, such as Carpe Donut or Barefoot Bucha.

Perhaps most of all, it's a Charlottesville signature. First-year students at the university place excited phone calls to parents, telling them about the bustling parking lot downtown where they spent—and ate away—most of their Saturday morning. Young professionals bring home gifts of sage and pork sausage for the holidays, informing their families about the vendor from whom they purchased their breakfast. People from different counties, social backgrounds and professions all show up on Saturday mornings—or Wednesday and Thursday evenings—to partake in the ritual of buying groceries direct from vendors.

Stephanie Andregg-Maloy, current manager of the City Market, has been almost single-handedly responsible for the market's success and relevancy in the twenty-first century. When she came on board in 2003, the market was much smaller, with forty to fifty vendors. She wanted part-time work and hadn't realized the city ran the market, given that it wasn't well advertised and there was no visible structure. The thought of improving the market was interesting to Andregg-Maloy, and its Saturday-based work allowed for time with her son.

The market, more than anything, needed organizational skills and management skills. She wanted the market to be "more of a business than a chaotic gathering."[92] The first month was chaos—non-reserve vendors would just show up and make lines on First Street. People would arrive at 1:00 or 2:00 a.m. and sleep in their cars in order to get a spot. It didn't make sense for farmers, given that "stuff will go bad." Farmers lined up for visibility and business, which the central location in a parking lot on Water Street downtown enabled. This spot on Water Street has been "in transition" and "temporary" for many years, which causes "anxiety for the vendors because of spatial insecurity." Though numerous city meeting and citizen petitions have ensued, the City Market has remained in the same spot, albeit a "temporary one," since 1993. Andregg-Maloy allows that while the market has always had a good reputation, it's only gotten better.

Andregg-Maloy's priorities for the current market are produce, fruits and prepared foods. Andregg-Maloy is quick to point out that while the Charlottesville City Market has changed over the years, it still remains true to Cason's vision of a place where farmers sell their produce locally. Today, farmers compose 45 percent of the vendors, selling produce, including fruits, vegetables and cut greenery; live plants; herbs; flowers; meat; poultry; eggs; and dairy products. The farmers' market also operates on Wednesday in Meade Park and Tuesday in the Forest Lakes neighborhood on Route 29, as well as smaller offshoots in the UVA hospital parking lot or around town on various days.

The occasionally high price of local goods and the well-off customer these goods normally attract have not escaped Andregg-Maloy. Since 2003, she has made it a priority to involve, not target, additional groups than the "higher class customer" who usually frequents the market. The City Market has replaced its acceptance of "local currency" with EBT cards, an initiative started by JABA in connection with its self-improvement classes. The market also interacts with Children, Youth and Family Services; Market Central is set to take over the EBT relationship in 2013. Her increased efforts to enfold more of the Charlottesville community into the vibrant local food scene will only meet increased success over the next several seasons.

The kinds of grocery retailers in the Charlottesville-Albemarle area, whether gourmet or homegrown, vary in quantity and kind. Latin food marts thrive several blocks away from the Meade Park market on Wednesday; Feast! does a solid business one street away from the affordable and popular Reid Super-Save. Whether through EBT cards, smaller packages of produce or even stands alongside roadways, retailers in Charlottesville are dedicated to getting local ingredients to a variety of home cooks eager to transform this bounty into first-rate meals. Pancetta from Olli Salumeria renders into

Downtown Charlottesville at dusk. *Photo by Sean Michael McCord.*

Thomas Jefferson's estate, Monticello. *Photo by Christopher Hollis for Wdwic Pictures.*

Peter Hatch in his garden in Crozet. *Photo by Kevin Haney.*

Michie Tavern. *Photo by Purple Flower.*

Laying hens at Free Union Grass Farm. *Photo by Kevin Haney.*

Donnie Montgomery's Stoneybrook Farm, one of two dairies that supply milk to Homestead Creamery. *Photo by Nancy Overton.*

Pastured chickens at Timbercreek Organics. *Photo by Casey Ireland.*

The brood herd at Timbercreek Organics. *Photo by Casey Ireland.*

A flock of geese at Free Union Grass Farm. *Photo by Kevin Haney.*

Zach and Sara Miller with their children, Emory and Sanders. *Photo by Casey Ireland.*

A curious kid at Caromont Farm. *Photo by Casey Ireland.*

A batch of Red Row cheeses aging at Caromont. *Photo by Casey Ireland.*

Kate Collier, co-owner of Feast! *Photo by Kevin Haney.*

Acorn squash, sweet potatoes and onions supplied by the Local Food Hub. *Photo by Kevin Haney.*

Will Richey cutting up a Timbercreek Organics chicken in the Whiskey Jar's kitchen. *Photo by Casey Ireland.*

Walking between vendors at the City Market. *Photo by Kevin Haney.*

Harrison Keevil and his cookbook collection at Brookville. *Photo by Kevin Haney.*

The downstairs bar at the C&O. *Photo by Kevin Haney.*

C&O's old-fashioned cocktail. *Photo by Kevin Haney.*

Matt Rohdie and his children, Finn, Georgia and Lil, of Carpe Donut. *Photo by Casey Ireland.*

Sauvignon blanc grapes at Barboursville Vineyards. *Courtesy of Luca Paschina.*

A revision of Thomas Jefferson's vineyards at Monticello. *Photo by Tony Fischer for Thomas Jefferson, Horticulturist.*

Harvesting grapes at Trump Winery. *Courtesy of Kerry Woolard.*

A handful of hops at Starr Hill. *Photo by Kevin Haney.*

Above: Empty bottles at Starr Hill Brewery in Crozet. *Photo by Kevin Haney.*

Right: Mark Thompson, owner of Starr Hill, pouring a pint. *Photo by Kevin Haney.*

Bottles of cider waiting to be labeled on-site at Potter's Craft Cider. *Courtesy of Tim Edmond.*

Timbercreek Organics' piglets at eight weeks old. *Photo by Casey Ireland.*

A selection of Olli Salame. *Photo by Kevin Haney.*

crisp pieces for a rich amatriciana sauce, while collard greens cook down deliciously with local onions and Berkshire bacon from Edward's Ham. Salads, sauces, crumb cakes and cordials are all made tastier and more honest with the addition of local ingredients bought by local retailers from local farmers.

Farmers' markets, gourmet grocery stores and CSAs are all wonderful tools for the home cook—assuming that the food-minded individual enjoys or is capable of whipping up meals. Charlottesville's chefs frequent the City Market on Saturday morning, swapping cooking tips and picking up the freshest of ingredients before sleepy college students and hungry toddler-toting parents arrive on the scene. They work through the Local Food Hub for bulk onions and contact foragers in Staunton for ramps and mushrooms. These are even more resourceful and curious than the Charlottesville home cook, eager to transform the top of each season's—if not each week's—produce and the finest of local agricultural products into feasts fit for a president.

Chapter 4

Charlottesville Dining

How Lowbrow Sustenance Becomes Highbrow Meals (or Vice Versa)

Dining at the Farm and on the Field: Current Trends in Charlottesville Restaurants

As alluring as luscious, deep-purple plums and bundles of wiry scallions appear to the home cook at the City Market, seeing those items transformed on a clean white plate at a local restaurant is an arguably grander experience. Whether self-taught or trained at some of the most well-known culinary institutes in the world, chefs in Charlottesville truly know how to bring out the best in local ingredients. Weekly, if not daily, menu changes; prime seasonal ingredients; and personal relationships with farms and food producers characterize locavore-friendly spots in the area. Housed in old barns, tucked away in warehouse buildings or lofted up above the Downtown Mall, local-food restaurants in Charlottesville appear in all shapes, sizes and price points. Chicken tortilla soup, chock-full of the meaty shreds of birds from Timbercreek Organics, rings in at five dollars for an inexpensive lunch option at Revolutionary Soup; the same bird, dissembled and roasted at the Local, could cost a diner upward of twenty dollars. But the textures, smells and colors of local food as interpreted by a thoughtful chef at either diner or fine dining are worth a customer's consideration and dollars.

An increasingly visible character in pop culture and the culinary arts is the ardent locavore diner, one whose enthusiasm for local foodstuffs borders on the rabid. Viewers of *Portlandia* or *Saturday Night Live* are familiar with the

The matchbooks at the C&O Restaurant. *Photo by Kevin Haney.*

customer so invested in the origin of a meal, he or she travels to the farm in order to see firsthand how the animal has lived and died. The character is an understandable one, as there is something seductive, if not addictive or necessary, about tracking visible connections between the fork and the farm. The humorous characterization of the inquisitive diner stems in part from a very real panic many Americans are beginning to experience: the anxiety of having no knowledge or understanding of the places, stories or even animals behind the meals we eat.

Too often, the only animals that diners see are the cows dangling from Chick-fil-A billboards or the dancing chickens of Pollos Hermanos on *Breaking Bad*. The industrialization of farming, the accessibility of fast food and the rise of the supermarket have all contributed to an extreme level of disconnect between the consumed and the consumer. While CSAs, farmers' markets and alternative supermarkets allow the health and environmentally conscious to stock their homes with local products, these customers often want that same level of control and understanding when dining outside of the home or farm.

Charlottesville is home to many offerings for diners committed to various levels or conceptions of locavorism, as well as offerings for those for whom a good meal is simply that. A popular catchphrase among Charlottesvillians is how the city has more restaurants per square mile than New York City. While the most recent ReCount survey conducted by the NPD Group situates

Charlottesville between Portland and San Francisco as the fourteenth most restaurant-filled per capita city in the United States, the excitement and pride behind the restaurant scene in Charlottesville remains the same.[93] For, after all, what does a city like New York City offer diners that Charlottesville cannot? Accessible late-night options, ethnic hotspots, a variety of cuisines and an even bigger variety of brilliant chefs mark this small city as a culinary powerhouse. Why else would the *New York Times* document ways to spend—and eat—twenty-four hours in Charlottesville[94] or *Southern Living* write up a tour of chef turned producer Gail Hobbs-Page's home?[95] Charlottesville food has been influenced by the health-conscious simplicity of California cooking, the inquisitive inventiveness of New York and the back-to-our-roots southern charm of Charleston.

Current trends of heritage cooking, seasonal meals, strict regionality and more efficient methods of using ingredients have been well utilized in Charlottesville. It's still easy to find a perfectly cooked rib-eye in the city, but less traditional cuts such as tongue, hanging tenderloin and marrow have been appearing on menus. A proliferation of New Southern restaurants brings the taste of childhood and roadside stops in the Carolinas to the area, with the flavors of pimento cheese and pork belly. Yet despite the in-status of fried chicken and ham hocks, there are plenty of West Coast–inspired stops for a more health-conscious—and waistline-friendly—meal. Bowls of delicately scented *pho*, see-through vegetable rolls, light curries and crisp salads are mainstays around town for those looking to eat well and live well. For a town of its size and location in the Virginia countryside, Charlottesville offers diners trends *and* taste.

Though a focus on regionality, seasonality and sustainability has entered the culinary arena, Charlottesville's roots in a more European epicurean tradition still remain a powerful source of inspiration. Veal sweetbreads in a Madeira cream sauce, house-made charcuterie and artisanal cheese plates with selections from France and the United Kingdom abound at many fine-dining restaurants. Foundational sauces borrowed from French *haute cuisine*, Northern Italian pasta dishes and flambéed desserts sit comfortably on the menus of many restaurants still successful after the wave of Alice Waters–inspired cooking. The steak *chinoise* at C&O Restaurant, with its creamy tamari sauce and traditional presentation, is a classic Charlottesville meal alongside a Riverside cheeseburger or a bagel from Bodo's.

One of Charlottesville's greatest culinary successes is its ability to combine the highbrow with the lowbrow, its success with turning local bounty into gourmet excellence. One may pay over $100 for a full meal at

Palladio, but the beets in a delicate salad or the filling for plump agnolotti come from farms merely miles away. Perfectly seasoned trout at C&O was pulled out of the streams at Rag Mountain, while both imported San Marzano tomatoes and Rock Barn pork make up a thick ragù at Tavola. The freshest and most unique products at the City Market, farm stand or backyard garden are liquified, sautéed, mashed, grilled or preserved in ways both surprising and comforting.

In recent years, the craze and demand for local food has seemed to have moved from the high to lower classes, whereas the history of self-sustaining food production seems to be the opposite. Gail Hobbs-Page, former chef and current cheesemaker, has found that "southerners grab onto that way of living" in terms of localized, crafted food on account of "olfactory memory and traditions that were handed down or perhaps coming out of poverty." She muses, "I think we're just coming back to what genetically feels like home," whether that means backyard tomatoes instead of hothouse hybrids or cooking from-scratch mashed potatoes for the first time.[96] The instance of Sotheby's selling off heirloom vegetables for $1,000 translates onto the dinner table as well, with groups such as Outstanding in the Field offering sit-down dinners on local farms for upward of $200 per person.

The concept of sitting down for a fine meal in the midst of a working farm or cornfield is a study in contrasts. The earthiness and the rusticity of the setting belies the sophistication of the meal, no matter how humble its components. Corn from the field arrives dusted in chipotle pepper powder and liberally sprinkled with Cotija cheese, street food gone gourmet. A herd of cattle heard lowing in the background breaks down into a rather pricey selection of meat options; to put it simplistically, a diner will often pay more for the most simply and naturally raised product. Whether the item is carrots from a certified-organic operation or free-range duck, the challenges of farming and farming sustainably are costs passed on from the farmer to the diner when the farm's product goes to the restaurant.

But perhaps the acts of cooking and assembling ingredients to make a dish and then a meal are inventive processes that deserve a diner's attention—and their money. Chefs, bakers and food artisans in Charlottesville understand the culinary arts so well, transforming their acts of creation into a form of alchemy. Humble sauvignon blanc grapes, dusted in a smoky gray bloom, become a crisp, pale green wine at Veritas Vineyard. This sauvignon blanc, in turn, gets paired with fresh fish from the Chesapeake Bay, lovely on its own but turned flaky and flavorful with brown butter and almonds. Chefs of Charlottesville understand the power of the understated and the unexpected, whether it be tiny rosemary blossoms scattered on zucchini shavings or a perfectly fried potato. These are chefs taught by southern grandmothers, French chefs at ski resorts or Julia Child on TV. Their methodologies and flavors represent current movements in the restaurant world, but their personalities and stories are uniquely Virginian and particular to Charlottesville.

Slow Food Made Fast: Will Richey's Culinary Empire

Will Richey, with his homesteader lifestyle and antebellum fashion sense, is one of the most visible and well loved of these culinary characters. Known for his appreciation of both good food and good times, the man who runs Red Row Farm with his family was first known in the area for making really excellent soup. Richey's ownership of Revolutionary Soup and transformation of the punky soup stops into locavore hotspots preceded his founding of the Whiskey Jar, a southern restaurant known for hearty fare and many selections of the eponymous beverage. Richey started off in the area as a UVA student holding wine tastings and then became a cook at L'étoile, a French restaurant with an interest in Virginian history. He purchased Revolutionary Soup, which had only been open three hours a day and run by "punk kids," in 2005 at his wife's urging. In 2012, Richey directed his interests into running his farm and running the Whiskey Jar with his partners.

A dedication to local food and southern food has informed all of Richey's food endeavors. Though Richey is the third owner of Revolutionary Soup, he's "the first to take it in the local food aspect that it is."[97] The two restaurants, located downtown and on the Corner near UVA, are examples of slow food done fast. Hearty stews, delicate broths, filling salads and creative sandwiches have inspired "a dedicated local following, and because of that, we get tourists." Richey has found that most of his customer base is "a core local office group of people who want to eat healthy and want to eat well who believe in local foods." In comparison, Richey states, "Whiskey Jar is two restaurants in one": both family-friendly dining and a popular bar. The food at the Whiskey Jar is down-home and surprisingly traditional, with chickory salads and barbecued rabbit served alongside hush puppies and pecan pie. The restaurant gets tourists as well as "regular people who want to learn the whiskeys." Many customers come in for live music, though to Richey, the most interesting people are the people coming in for the food.

Steve Zissou and a collection of spirits along the brick walls of the Whiskey Jar's bar. *Photo by Kevin Haney.*

Richey was raised eating good food and always liked to go to restaurants, even starting tasting groups in college. Working at a wine shop was his first foray into a career as a gourmand before getting a job at L'étoile; according to Richey, working at that restaurant "was the life-changer." Richey was interested in gourmet food before local food; his interests began with the "French thing and fancy food. Food at its finest." Richey tells how Mark Reskey, owner of L'étoile, was a big Virginia history buff, interested in culinary questions like, "How can we re-create what the colonialists were eating?" Reskey did research at Monticello and created meals based on that. "It was definitely home," Richey admits.

The questions of "Who am I?" and what home tastes like underlie much of Richey's culinary philosophy. "My family's from the South," he states. "We're Virginians." With a laugh, Richey tells happy stories of "cooking with old ladies." While he may have "learned professional cooking from friends," Richey attests that his best recipes are his mother's. "I prefer the food eaten by my people," Richey admits, despite being a self-confessed Francophile with a love of fine wines and gourmet offerings. "I wanted it to be a lifestyle, tracking heirloom varieties. How did we lose that?" Richey muses. "We've lost that in all aspects of the culture—now it's homogenized and generic."

The ingredients and offerings at both Revolutionary Soup locations and at the Whiskey Jar, as well as the ways in which Richey sources his materials, are anything but basic. The percentage of local ingredients he uses at all three restaurants falls down to 50 percent in winter though tops at 80 percent in summer. They purchase local meats all year long; all the proteins at Whiskey Jar are local, and almost all at Revolutionary Soup are local. Richey is influenced by Anson Mills, a Charleston company that is also a big supporter of Southern Foodways Alliance. Richey and his cooks try to preserve a lot of summer produce, at times filling freezers with the last of summer's tomato pulps. Richey's goal for the future of his restaurants is increased organization, turning the Corner kitchen into a canning location.

When Richey's restaurants can't get local, they at least try to get organic. "I don't want to overstate what we do because then it belittles the good things

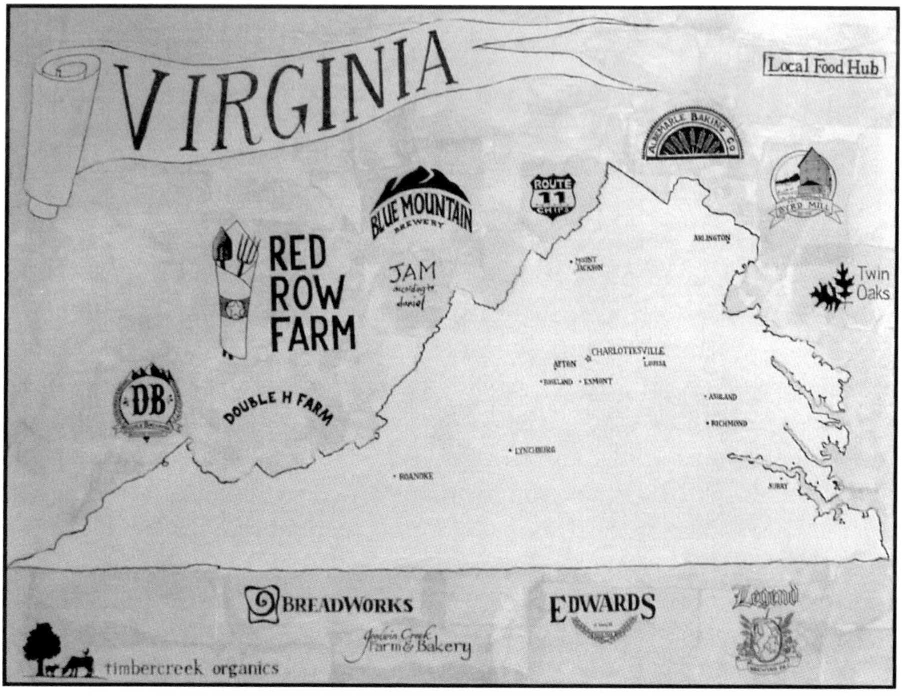

The map of local products at Revolutionary Soup. *Photo by Kevin Haney.*

we do," he attests. "Local dairy would kill you price-wise; we go through so much butter. At home, it's buy the good stuff, eat less of it, save other places." Part of Richey's ability to keep overhead down is his use of large-scale food distribution companies to his advantage. Richey has "made a lot of ground with Sysco" due to a rep who allows Richey to pursue his locavore interests, telling him, "I can source certain local things for you," like Byrd Mill, Edward's Ham products and Virginia peanuts. Both a self-confessed "Gen-X anti-establishmentarian" and an optimist, Richey has faith that one can get big institutions to work for the community, not vice versa.

Chefs like Will Richey, both powerfully individualistic thinkers and savvy businessmen, understand the ideological and financial benefits of working local ingredients into existing food systems. Yet there also exist alongside these practical restaurateurs iconoclasts who would rather rid society of current methods of food production and distribution than recuperate them. If local food is a spectrum, with one end being a fast-food burger joint and the other being a snack of sun-ripened berries eaten in one's own garden, Brookville Restaurant rests closer to the latter side of the scale. Harrison Keevil, chef and co-owner, understands and anticipates the desires of serious locavores interested in tracing the heritage and history of their meals.

Heritage Eating and Locavore Sensibilities

Born and bred in Virginia, Keevil proudly asserts himself as a "Virginia boy" shaped through travels in England and San Francisco.[98] "In London and San Francisco, the local food movement just got driven into my head," Keevil says. "I knew that there was a local food movement in Virginia because I worked on one of the first certified organic working farms in Virginia called Brookview Farm out in Goochland," Keevil notes. "I was familiar with the practices of sustainably raised meats and eggs and produce, and it was already kind of ingrained in me, even though I didn't quite know it yet." The realization of Keevil's farm-to-table dreams is an inviting space on the upstairs floor of a downtown space, with stretching timber beams and a welcoming atmosphere. "We just want people to feel comfortable, as if they were in their own kitchen because that's when you get the best conversations," Keevil says of Brookville's ambiance. "There's no VIPs here. It's like fine dining in your home."

And the dining is fine, indeed. Brookville's menu changes daily, though local ingredients—and lots of pork products—are always a guarantee. Crisp bacon, tender rabbit, handmade pasta and surprising vegetable combinations are hallmarks of Keevil's cooking. The food is both imaginative and familiar, with comfort foods such as burgers, fried chicken and BLTs redone for even more flavor and sensation. Warm chocolate chip cookies are studded with bacon bits for a pleasing savoriness; beef chili gets a dusting of cinnamon for additional depth. Seasonality is a given, as Keevil sources 95 percent of his products from Virginia. Seasonings like salt, pepper, sugar and spices, as well as oils and citruses, are imported by necessity; otherwise, Keevil likes to keep it strictly local. As a general rule, Keevil refuses to buy products not from the state. "I won't bring in salmon because someone wants a piece of salmon," Keevil attests. "If it doesn't grow in our soil, graze on our grass or swim in the Chesapeake Bay or in our rivers, we don't use it."

A look at the pork-heavy Brookville menu shows that Keevil is not shy about using meat in his dishes. Carnivorous dishes like bacon-wrapped foot-long hot dogs, Surry sausage sandwiches and egg and bacon sliders are available for feasting—and these are only appetizers. However, diners can expect more than rib-eyes or pork tenderloins from Keevil when dining at his restaurant. "We do focus a lot on nose to tail, the other bits," he states. At Brookville, "other bits" can mean anything from pork belly to whole chickens. His attitude toward meat and toward food in general is almost New Age in its consideration of each ingredient's and animal's significance. "It's our belief that these animals died for us to be nourished and fed, so it's my job to respect that animal and use as much of the animal as I can," Keevil attests. "They were treated amazingly well when they were alive, and it was their job to become food for us, so it's my job to make them shine on the plate and show they did not live a meaningless life." With items like three-quarter-pound burgers served with bacon marmalade at Brookville, it's hard to imagine an animal feeling anything less than content with its lot as dinner.

His insistence on local sourcing and commitment to finding new ways to present Virginia-produced ingredients make a chef like Keevil a prime advocate and partner for farmers both small and large. Keevil easily rattles off producers, farms and individuals with whom Brookville has a direct relationship. There's beef, chicken, pork and eggs from Timbercreek Organic and produce from a variety of farms all over the area. There's lamb from Ottawa Farms and seafood from Sam Rust Seafood, a family-owned business in Virginia Beach, so Keevil can rest assured that "any of the fish [Brookville gets] in has been Virginia-landed on Virginia boats by Virginia fishermen."

To Keevil and his wife, Jennifer, who co-owns the restaurant and manages the front of the house, farmers are both business associates and friends. "We pick up the phone ten, twenty times a day talking to individual people, saying, 'How are you, how's the family?' and then we get down to business because we have a personal relationship with them, not just a business relationship with them," Keevil states. In his mind, the occupations of the farmer and the restaurateurs are intermingled, if not mutually dependent. Regardless of friendships, the future of Brookville depends on the growth of Virginia agriculture. To Keevil, "The business relationship definitely leads [Brookville] into being loyal and wanting them to succeed just as much as we are because if they don't succeed, we can't succeed."

It's worth examining the fact that Charlottesville's most local restaurant is also among the city's more expensive dining options. Most dinner entrées clock in at over eighteen dollars per plate, with its decadent burger costing twenty-two dollars. Brunch items and lunch options are not exorbitantly priced yet cost a diner significantly more than a Bodo's bagel or donut from Spudnuts. Though Keevil and his wife practice what they preach and maintain an accessible, non-pretentious atmosphere, the average customer at Brookville is not the average American diner. The prices at Brookville, quite simply, are a reflection and continuation of the prices of local, sustainably raised ingredients, which, in turn, reflect the costs and labors of farmers invested in alternative agriculture. In order to provide the most local, freshest and most vibrant ingredients from nearby farms and producers, the food costs and thus food prices at Brookville are often above average.

Regardless of price, all these dumplings, sweet potatoes and pork bellies make a diner question whether Virginia-local equates southern heritage foods of the Elvis Presley persuasion. The state's natural growing season, historically grown food crops and particularly multifaceted cooking heritage all contribute to a popular conception that food harvested and produced from a southern area is best made into southern food. Yet while a chicken may be from a nearby farm, if it's marinated in buttermilk, dredged in flour and cayenne and fried in its own fat, the taste of local can get confused with the taste of a greasy spoon. Chefs such as Dean Maupin at the C&O Restaurant finesse popular local ingredients into *haute cuisine*. His particular brand of French-American cuisine is almost a direct throwback to Jefferson's culinary preferences, or at least an era when good taste and good food was synonymous with European flair.

European Traditions in Fine Dining

The C&O is arguably one of Charlottesville's most exceptional and beautiful restaurants, as well as one of its most well known. Part gallery space, part restaurant, the C&O is pieced together from several floors, units and terraces of a former railway station to create a space of elegant rusticity. A huge, handmade hardwood bar stretches across a first-floor room, trimmed with pine plank walls and an orderly beverage display. The warmth and intimacy of the downstairs bar continues onto the second-floor dining area, while the top floor's nook of a dining room is more formal, with views looking out over downtown Charlottesville. A knowledgeable waitstaff, bartenders-cum-DJs and a creative kitchen make C&O both a dependable local watering hole and a fine dining destination.

On first impression, Dean Maupin could be a bassist in a New Wave band instead of a chef trained by French imports in ski resort kitchens. A native of Crozet, Maupin cut his teeth in the apprenticeship program at the Greenbrier Hotel in West Virginia. Rotations on breakfast shifts, sauce shifts and multiple other departments allowed for intensive training in various aspects of cooking for fine dining. Stints at Albemarle Baking Company and the Boar's Head Inn preceded Maupin's tenure at the C&O, an originally French restaurant opened in 1976.

A father of three, Maupin's ownership of the C&O is informed by his family life and vice versa, like many other food producers and chefs in the area. Maupin views restaurant work as the means to stay outside the mainstream nine-to-five work culture but insists on making his job work for his family. "The beauty of independent restaurants is that we close on holidays, but it's counterculture in that sense where you're going to work when everyone is getting off," Maupin says.[99] Having other cooks in the household doesn't hurt, either. "My wife was a chef, and she did this for ten years, working her way into good kitchens," he notes. "She understands the time commitment and dedication it takes." Maupin's twenty-year career at C&O has certainly demanded dedication on his part; like any successful individual, however, Maupin has managed to balance work and family in a way that has made both intrinsic to his daily life.

The C&O's current mix of French and American cuisines, liberally peppered with local ingredients and seasonal flavors, was not always so. According to Maupin, C&O in its original format was as old school and traditional as some of Thomas Jefferson's classic French recipes. Maupin states, "It wasn't until the very early 2000s when the C&O stopped doing the French menu upstairs." The more formal dining room on the second floor was almost a separate restaurant from the first floor, referred to as "the Bistro." "One menu upstairs was French food, handwritten in French, with different plates than the Bistro but the same systems," Maupin relates. "It needed to become a convivial, simplified menu." And simplify Maupin has. C&O classics such as the steak *chinoise*, butter lettuce salad with Pommery mustard vinaigrette and the delectable *coupe maison* remain on the menu but in updated forms with new accompaniments. The classic salad now comes with grated Gruyère; the *coupe* is now topped with whipped white chocolate, with strawberries added to the decadent sundae.

When asked what makes Maupin's restaurant distinct from other fine dining options in the area, he notes that individuality and experience are key. "We're all pulling from the same pool of vendors and farmers so that what makes you different is not so much the product that you're using but the experience you're offering," Maupin says. "I think there's great-quality food all over Charlottesville, which is truly a unique thing, this town being as saturated as it is with talented people and people who want to eat that way." According to the chef, the only distinguishing factor between himself and other chefs are his "personal experiences as a chef and their personal experiences as a chef, how I look at it, how I write a menu, the relationships that I have with my line cooks." Maupin sees running a restaurant as a collaborative experience, viewing himself as equally important as the line cooks and servers who implement his culinary designs. Another integral part of the collaborative effort is the products of local food providers.

To Maupin, seasonal agriculture and local produces affects both his "psyche as a chef" and the business itself. He admits that while "it's not like we go dormant in those months that the local economy is not producing the abundance for us," C&O does "try to get creative with it." Buying local produce does increase food costs for the restaurant. Maupin has found that "it's not cheaper than the stuff we ship from California or Florida," yet he continues to average at about 60–70 percent local ingredients year-round because of its ideological importance to Maupin. "I've learned to flow with the seasons," he says. "I know what's available now. I spend a lot more money now because I try to pull in as much as I can from the Food Hub or whoever is calling up."

The C&O has particular loyalties to certain local producers, such as trout from Rag Mountain. "Do I feel like every week when Ellen calls, I should get sixty or seventy? Yeah, because the place has been doing it for twenty-five years," Maupin says. He has bought produce from Manakintowne Specialty

Growers every week since becoming a chef in Charlottesville, though he has been increasingly using the Local Food Hub's. "Caromont's cheese is a staple," Maupin states, as are mushrooms from Sharondale Farm and the foraging efforts of locals. Maupin lists with ease his various meat providers—Retreat Farm for lamb, Best of What's Around for beef, Polyface for pork and chickens. "Those places have thrived for many years around here," he notes, "but we certainly have a lot of relationships with a lot of local businesses."

Maupin's transformation of the C&O from fancy French dining to a local mainstay and Charlottesville gem is a lesson on adaptation and resourcefulness. While his kitchen may use many of the same products and ingredients as the Whiskey Jar and Brookville, Maupin's particular blend of locavore sensibility with a European culinary heritage makes his restaurant one-of-a-kind. Its varying levels of formality, intimate setting and inventive use of ubiquitous-seeming local fare all demonstrate the license that a creative chef can take with the best food products around.

From Pork Tacos to Pastries: Humble Food That's Local

Despite the successes of places like the C&O or Will Richey's food empire, not every chicken from Polyface Farms or scrap of pork from the Rock Barn goes to fine dining or even locavore dining. Local can be as easy as a fresh taco al pastor eaten out of a family-owned Mexican food truck or as simple as a still-warm donut. Matt Rohdie, a kind-spoken East Coast native who views Charlottesville as his unofficial hometown, has created a veritable food empire with his truck turned shop Carpe Donut. Rohdie's business is an example of a successful micro-enterprise, a shop that started small and ended up in Whole Foods. "Our dream was to make magically good donuts and sell them across the counter," Rohdie relates.[100] "We learned the donuts froze and rewarmed beautifully, which opened up tons of opportunities. One of the event planners whom I had worked with asked for a donut cart at a wedding, which gave us a financial base and whole new market." Rohdie views Carpe Donut first as "a catering company, then a shop, then a street vendor."

What exactly makes Carpe Donut, initially a single-product business, so tasty and so successful? Rohdie defines his clove-scented cider donut as "organic comfort food, the kinds of food people grew up eating and wanted to eat." His desire to provide a fun product that nourishes its eater stems

An apple cider donut from Carpe Donut. *Photo by Casey Ireland.*

from his attachment to his family. "I want to make food for Charlottesville the way I make food for my kids," Rohdie says. Like local homesteaders and family farmers, Rohdie and his wife began their business as a way to stay closer to home and children. After reading Laura Ingalls Wilder's *Little House on the Prairie* books to his daughter, Rohdie realized that the family in the story "spent all day together. It was only 140 years ago," he muses. "How did we lose that?" His current occupation makes it easy for his family to understand his job, which is simply that "Daddy makes donuts."

If the quality of food items bought at Carpe Donut is any indication of the way the Rohdie family eats, one only wishes they could take a seat at that dinner table. Bracing kombucha from Barefoot Bucha, spiced apple cider and a mouth-coating Italian hot chocolate so thick that it resembles ganache are beverages available to customers who buy a single or several dozen donuts. The fried dough rings themselves are surprisingly flavorful and dense, filled with spice and just eggy enough. The donuts are magical to eat, easily savored until the last taste of cinnamon-sugar coating gets licked off of fingertips. The donut cart's location in the UVA amphitheater in 2012 brightened up January afternoons for many students who sat in old libraries, scooping remnants of hot chocolate out of small paper cups and dusting crumbs off of books and laps.

Like Will Richey of Revolutionary Soup and the Whiskey Jar, Rohdie's shop is "a secret advocate for organic and sustainable food." With glee, he relates how a mother, upon reading the shop's list of ingredients, will tell her child, "Okay, you can have one donut." According to Rohdie, a diner can taste the difference in local, organic and sustainably raised ingredients when only five are used in the entire product. Donuts at Carpe Donut are surprisingly seasonal. The main impact on the shop comes from cider and eggs. Carpe Donut gets its cider from Pennsylvania when the local cider production stops. The local supply from nearby orchards constitutes four months' worth of cider, though Rohdie freezes up to three more months' worth before going regional. In the past couple years, the pastured egg supply has been essentially constant. The shop is always on the lookout for more local ingredients, particularly flour. "The localness of food can get exquisite," Rohdie notes. "I've expanded my definition to include local production of food." Carpe Donut is returning to frying the donuts in organic palm fruit oil, which is, as a non-GMO product, six times more expensive than soybean oil.

Donut shops and small businesses are not the only ways in which locavore interests have been made less fancy. If local food started as an upper-class movement, one specific to the highly educated or those with disposable incomes, its success has not gone unnoticed by the corporate and the everyday. "Greenwashing" has become as commonplace in restaurants as it has in grocery stores, with seemingly everyone in the business trying to get their thumbs in the locavore pie. Chipotle Mexican Grill, a popular chain of southwestern restaurants, claims to serve "food with integrity." Integrity, for Chipotle, involves incorporating local products into its menu along with antibiotic-free meats and recycled napkins. Its actual practice of sourcing local food, however, can be somewhat more opaque.

On its website, Chipotle declares its interest in and support of local foods, noting that "there are many ways to define" what makes an ingredient local, subscribing to a 350-mile radius when sourcing local produce. The very fact that a company as large as Chipotle, with over 1,500 locations in North America and Europe, includes local foods as a business mission is decidedly new and forward thinking. However, the amount of local foods that make up the menu at any given Chipotle is neither disclosed by the business nor easily accessible to curious diners. Adriana Hill, manager of the Charlottesville

Chipotle on Emmett Street, says that "the only local ingredient that [Chipotle uses] is the *carnitas*...from Polyface," noting that the company tells employees to "not answer any questions, no surveys, no interviews, unless it's coming from within Chipotle Corporate."[101] Additionally, Louisa Nickel, a customer service consultant for Chipotle, says that the company "currently [does] not have any local suppliers for produce in the Charlottesville area."[102] While Chipotle may offer customers reasonably priced fast food in an inventive setting, Charlottesville diners expecting local food consistently from the chain would be wiser to choose Chipotle's food for other reasons.

Fast-food chains are not the only players in the corporate food industry to stake out territory in the locavore scene. Will Richey of Revolutionary Soup and the Whiskey Jar tells a story of a trip to Washington, D.C., that ended up with a visit to a D.C./Maryland franchise offering a farm-to-table dining experience. Richey relates his excitement in finding local food in a corporatized setting, only to be disappointed with a lack of information. "I asked, 'Where is your chicken from?' and the server couldn't tell me," Richey says. "I said, 'How do you get your greens?' and no one knew." The big claims and unclear background of places like this franchise have led Richey not to advertise his restaurants as locavore-friendly. To Richey, it's "become a little ridiculous to try and tout it now as 'I'm more local, no, I'm more local!' I count on my customers to do the talking."

THE FUTURE OF LOCAVORE DINING

To many chefs, the survival of local food as an entrenched concept rather than a trend depends on its increased affordability. Will Richey sees the movement failing "if it's a gourmet-only option," acknowledging that local food is always "going to be more expensive." Richey still receives negative feedback about prices being too high at Revolutionary Soup and the Whiskey Jar; however, his businesses "get a lot of people who are like, 'How can you do it for that cheap?'" Richey states that his businesses "take a hit on our margin to make it in volume, and that's our secret. I'd rather do fifty people at half the price." Between the under-ten-dollar offerings of Revolutionary Soup and the accessible price points of chicken-and-dumplings or big breakfasts at the Whiskey Jar, Richey has certainly made a name for himself doing local for less.

Other cooks think that prices aren't the only variables that can change for more customers to buy local. Matt Rohdie believes that customers should expand their definition of local from the "exquisitely" minute to include local food production. To Rohdie, a large company using one product from the area isn't enough to make that company a viable support to the community. "At Chipotle, a tiny fraction of my money stays local; most goes back to Chipotle Corporate National," Rohdie attests. "Little localities should be able to reject the corporate forces that drive up prices and don't put money back into the community." With a laugh, Rohdie says that the lettuce on a Philly cheesesteak doesn't matter—it's the authenticity of the sandwich that counts. "I consider that cheesesteak [from Lou's] as local as a container of lettuce from Planet Earth Diversified," Rohdie insists.

Local food, however, can be greatly impacted by the beverage with which it's served. A pairing of Riesling with a flank steak, or a Syrah with flounder, can negatively alter one's perception of a meal's greatness. Just as a bottled Coke naturally suits a burger from Riverside Lunch, a bottle of local wine, when matched skillfully to a particular dish, elevates a meal to another level of perfection. With both the wine and beer industries in Virginia growing, the decision to drink local as well as eat local has become an increasingly popular and prevalent option for locavore diners who would rather not drink an imported white with their Timbercreek chicken.

Chapter 5

Virginia Vinoculture and Breweries

The Beginnings of Virginia Winemaking

A good chef understands the concept of "what grows together goes together." The decision to pair animals and vegetables that grew on the same soil on the same plate often results in a resonating, complex meal of regional refinement. The same principle can be applied to the pairing of local foods with local wines. The meatball special at Tavola, made of pork and beef from Timbercreek Organics, tastes even better with a bottle of Gabriele Rausse's Rosso; a mountain trout served with brown butter shines with a glass of mineral-rich Barboursville Riesling. Thanks to both good fortune as well as a historically motivated effort to establish an industry, central Virginia has developed a reputation for first-class wine and craft beers capable of matching the commonwealth's culinary excellence.

The story of Virginia wine is an old one, one that begins with European grapevines nurtured on Monticello soil. The numerous national awards given to Virginia wines, their success in state dinners and foreign markets and the surprising depth and variety of local offerings would have made Thomas Jefferson, Virginia's original oenophile, drunk with pride. Jefferson's love of the gourmet extended beyond French dinners and imported cheeses. In 1816, Jefferson acknowledged, "Habit [has] rendered the light and high flavored wines a necessary of life with me."[103] Having eschewed the heavily alcoholic and traditionally British ports and Madeiras, Jefferson looked to the French and Italians for inspiring his palate and his plans for a vineyard.

A taste for French and Italian wines was not the only oenological trend that Jefferson started in the United States. In the years prior to the War of 1812, Jefferson expressed an interest in promoting American wine as an alternate to European imports, largely due to a desire for political and cultural autonomy from Great Britain. Not only was foreign wine "among the earliest luxuries" in which colonial Americans "indulge[d]," Jefferson found it "desirable it should be made here."[104] The ideological allure of homegrown grapes and homegrown wines was matched by the seemingly practical reality of American climates and terroir. "We have every soil, aspect, & clime of the best wine countries," Jefferson attested, "and I have myself drank wines made in this state and in Maryland, of the quality of the best Burgundy."[105]

Modern oenophiles would argue that American wines need no comparisons to Old World bottles, but Jefferson's interest in staking a claim for New World vines proved a necessary first step for the evolution of Virginia wine. Jefferson himself planted two vineyards at Monticello, whose lack of success is indicated in the number of times Jefferson had to replant.[106] *Vitis vinifera*, the classic winemaking grape species in Europe, fared poorly against American enemies such as black rot and *phyloxera*.[107] Clever wildlife made meals out of the tender grapes, their juices providing easy nourishment instead of alcoholic pleasure.

Long sea journeys in the dark and rolling hold of a ship also proved fatal for many of the vine cuttings Jefferson sought to plant in his own vineyards. According to Gabriele Rausse, both a Monticello affiliate and a premier winemaker in the area, the import process provided one of the most elemental reasons for vineyard failure at the estate. Jefferson's vines were coming from Europe; given that there was no way to refrigerate them or to properly protect the vines, their unique vascular systems were often too damaged to be planted successfully upon arrival. Though perhaps more tenderness and careful study could have resurrected these broken vines, Jefferson's busy schedule and jack-of-all-trades variety of interests may have proved the final nail in the coffin for these early attempts at Virginia winemaking. In Rausse's opinion, Jefferson's vineyards failed mainly because "there was too much going on, there were other priorities." Ultimately, the juiciness of a pinot noir or the buttery richness of a Chardonnay were to be had with difficulty, if at all, at the vineyards of Jefferson's Monticello.

Native species of grapes offered more potential in terms of industrial production, yet the inferior quality of their wine made large-scale production undesirable. Jefferson had earlier praised the qualities of the southern muscadine *Vitis rotundifo* in the form of a North Carolinian scuppernog wine yet seemed reluctant to commit to using this grape or *Vitis labrusca*, the fox grape, as foundational vines for his fledgling vineyard.[108] The twenty-four grape varietals that made up the 1807 planting at Jefferson's estate were an amalgamation of popular choices and table grapes, representing "the vineyard of a plant collector, an experimenter rather than a serious wine maker."[109] The story of wine at Monticello is one of trial and error, an experiment by one of the premier epicureans of early America whose winemaking dreams—and mistakes—had set the stage for future successes.

Almost two centuries later, Jefferson's dreams of melding the taste of Italian wine with American industriousness became a reality on 120 acres of central Virginian red clay. Barboursville Vineyards, established in 1976 by Italian expat Gianni Zonin, is home to many "firsts" of the Virginia wine industry. Gabriele Rausse is also a renowned local vintner, having earned the moniker "father of Virginia wine" during his tenure at Barboursville in the 1970s. Barboursville Vineyards produced the first Virginia wines to be exported to China and provided the Bordeaux-style Octagon blend at the British Embassy's reception for Prince William's marriage to Kate Middleton in 2011.[110] The *New York Times* acknowledges that "Jefferson would have cheered" for the successes of Barboursville, finding that "the best of the Virginia wines are fresh, graceful, deeply colored and full of varietal character."[111]

Barboursville Vineyards rests on a picturesque 870-acre plot of land stretching from Albemarle to Orange County. The "romantic" red brick ruins of James Barbour's Neo-Palladian mansion, designed by Thomas Jefferson in 1822, now belong to the vineyard.[112] The octagonal projection of the house and its architectural ties to Jeffersonian innovation have proven clear influences on both owners and managers of Barboursville. Zonin purchased the property after a vacation in Charlottesville, attracted to both the geographic layout and the historical background of Barboursville. Luca Paschina, head winemaker at Barboursville, noted, "The history of the place, the Jefferson connection, the ruins all interested him. He's an Italian."[113]

It was Paschina's journey to the vineyard in 1990 as a consultant that marked Barboursville's ascendance to a higher quality of wine production. Polite and unassuming, Paschina admits that the vineyard has not changed dramatically since his arrival at the vineyard, stating, "The owner was focused since the beginning on producing the best wine we can from this land and therefore defining a wine region which did not exist."[114] Paschina confesses, "I pruned all winter long with the people here. They had no idea

Ruins of the Barboursville mansion on the property of Barboursville Vineyards. *Courtesy of the Historic American Buildings Survey.*

how to do it." Over time, Paschina and the team at Barboursville "built up our knowledge of the conditions here. Gradually better vines became available, and we learned which ones would do best."[115]

"Best," at Barboursville, is more than a relative statement from a modest winemaker. Particular varieties such as viognier and cabernet franc have done well in the red Piedmont soil, breathing New World life into trusty European varietals that had been previously imported. One of the key elements to the success has been the championing over, or at least truce with, Virginia's clime and wildlife. Dr. Tony Wolf, professor of viticulture at Virginia Tech, has noted that modern winemakers "have more tools in our management toolbox" than did Jefferson in the 1820s or even Zonin in the 1970s. Graelyn Brashear finds that "with pesticides and fungicides, growers can pamper a crop out of the fragile *vinifera* varieties that consumers know and seek out."[116]

Barboursville's place at the cornerstone of the Virginia wine industry tells a story of collaboration, the melding of several visions, strengths and histories for the creation of a solid and consistent product. The dreams of Jefferson, Zonin and Paschina have seemingly coalesced into an elegant and well-marketed bottle of cabernet franc, sampled in the large stone tasting room or purchased at the local Whole Foods. The tale of Gabriele Rausse, father of Virginia wine, is, by contrast, one of fierce individuality.

Big and Small Stories of Local Vintners

Gabriele Rausse's wines are sold under his name, papered with a simple brown label denoting the variety. His winery holds no tasting room, no area for customers to taste the wine or talk up the wine pourers. He has no website and no Facebook page hosting updates or offering space for enthusiasts to praise his vintages. His is a less accessible brand, a winemaker's wine intended for serious consumers. Underneath Rausse's warmth and easy laugh rests a distrust for mainstream food establishments, an almost utilitarian reliance on his own senses—and sensibility. "People are so willing to believe in anything somebody tells them," Rausse admits. "I believe only what I can see with my eyes and touch with my hands. Words for me don't mean much."[117]

Aging in oak barrels. *Photo by Kevin Haney.*

If one is to rely solely on taste, the solidity of Rausse's wines speaks for itself. According to Margaux and Company, a wine import company that represents Rausse, his wines "bear an unmistakable European stamp," offering a "clean structure, clear fruit flavors, judicious use of oak and realistic pricing."[118] His vineyard rests on a seven-acre plot, though most of the grapes that Rausse uses come from vineyards he has planted for other growers.[119] With his two sons, Rausse is responsible for the entire production of his wines. Easily accessible table blends, rarities such as *vin gris* and decadent Old World selections like *nebbiolo* characterize the Gabriele Rausse Winery offerings.

Well traveled and well educated, Rausse has a degree from the University de Milan in agricultural science, a degree "which trains you to be in charge of a farm with a lot of different crops." Part of Rausse's allure to the Barboursville founders was his experience with grape-growing in Italy, coupled with his experience in Australia with raising cattle and sheep. According to Rausse, the original thought behind Zonin's spur-of-the-moment purchase of Barboursville was that "if grapes don't work, we will do something else." He notes, "When the farm at Barboursville started, we bought cows, we bought horses, we started to grow soybeans and corn. We had no clue which direction to go and we were discouraged by VA Tech and USDA over and over."

Rausse worked as the general manager of Barboursville until 1981, when he left to help establish Simeon Vineyards, now named Jefferson Vineyards. In 1999, he aided the foundation of Kluge Estate Winery and Vineyard and consulted on Afton Mountain Vineyard, Blenheim, First Colony, Stone Mountain and White Hall.[120] In 1997, he left Jefferson Vineyard to come to Monticello "mainly because the offer he had was very attractive," and so he said, "If I have to work for free, I will do it for a nonprofit organization. The plan was to do something myself." He obtained his license under the agreement of renting Blenheim; Rausse took care of Blenheim for several years before Dave Matthews purchased the vineyard. He then planted his own vineyard in 1997, and then Kluge came on the scene. Rausse doesn't worry about planting more vines for himself because of his consulting jobs. The grapes for his wine come from all around Virginia, mainly *nebbiolo* and pinot noir varieties.

Rausse's wines, like the man himself, reveal an equal investment in restraint and pleasure. Rausse abhors commodified and over-branded food products, preferring the freshness of garden-picked figs to the fluorescent aisles of grocery stores. To Rausse, smaller is better, both as a winemaker and consumer. "They have regulations that we have in Virginia that we don't have in other states, so for me, I feel comfortable in using Virginia wines because I know what is going on in that wine," Rausse states. "I do prefer always the small grower for the simple reason that if he's small, he's not interested in money." A love of knowledge, distrust of large-scale production methods and constant urge for refinement and development mark Gabriele Rausse and his wines as singular in vision and refreshingly straightforward.

Rausse exists at one end of the spectrum of winemaking and wine marketing, relying on word of mouth and personal integrity to get the product to its target audience. If Barboursville, with its name recognition and international appeal, offers a glimpse at the potential market that Virginia wine may reach, Trump Winery takes its self-branding one step further. Donald Trump purchased the vineyard and facility of the defunct Kluge Estate Winery and Vineyard from Patricia Kluge in April 2012. Since opening in October of that year, Trump Winery has done a quick business of entrenching itself as a reputable—and lauded—producer of Virginia wine. In March 2013, *Wine Enthusiast* gave the Trump Winery SP Reserve a 91 rating, "the highest rating the magazine has ever given to any Virginia wine, still or sparkling."[121] Sold in three different countries, served at Chelsea Clinton's wedding and graced with the instant recognition of the Trump family name, Trump Winery offers consumers an entirely different product in a decidedly different package than Gabriele Rausse's minimalist presentation.

The tasting room at Trump Winery is almost always packed, filled with everyone from excited college students to well-dressed wine enthusiasts from Washington, D.C. A spacious outdoor patio, stone interiors and dark wood accents give the impression of an expensive mountain cabin. The wine, like the tasting room, is glamorous without ostentation. The only showy qualities on the wines' labels are the Trump name, just as the wine itself is made remarkable by its own solidity.

Kerry Woolard, general manager for the winery, finds that while "wineries in our area are after the same clients, mostly local people as well as the D.C. and Richmond crowd," the global nature of the Trump name makes the winery's reach "a little bit broader." Trump Winery has more success with wholesale business, as it is distributed in sixteen different states and three different countries.[122] Woolard acknowledges, "Virginia wine has been spread out further than it had been because of our distribution network."

The biggest assets to Trump Winery are its "size and global brand recognition." Woolard relates flying to various brand meetings, doing demos for distributors, visiting other Trump properties, engaging in staff training and winemakers' dinners and serving wine at members-only events. "Other wineries in Virginia are more reliant on people buying wine at wineries," she says. "The Trump wine is in other markets." Woolard notes that her demonstrations begin with a two-minute description of Virginia before she talks about the wine; to her, the Trump brand provides "a great opportunity to expose people all over the world to Virginia wine that wouldn't have had it in any other context or exposure."

Trump Winery's position in the heart of the Monticello Wine Trail attracts more serious wine consumers; Woolard finds that Charlottesville lends to that appeal. "I don't think the wine industry would have developed in the capacity it has if not for the culinary and farm-to-table aspects of Charlottesville," she states. Woolard believes wine and food to be mutually dependent, as it's "weird to go to a wine area without a culinary scene." Given that "the wine-interested traveler has interest in culinary experiences as well," Trump Winery seeks to provide visitors with a memorable, seasonal menu. The restaurant serves Caromont cheeses, Surryano ham and Monastery Gouda, with pork products coming from the Rock Barn. "I've always felt there is a disconnect between wine as a farm product," Woolard states. "Some of the best restaurants in Charlottesville have local products all over and no local wines." She sees wine in the bottle as often removed from the farm process but attests that Trump Winery is a local farm as well.

Trump Winery is "fortunate" to be in the Monticello American Viticultural Area (AVA), which is already known as the premier wine-growing area in the state. This AVA's general reputation for being serious about wine quality lends the vineyard "more history, more longevity, more wines" and the ability to be "taken more seriously." In 2012, the Governor's Cup picked out the top twelve wines to constitute a "governor's case"; eleven of the twelve were from grapes grown in the Monticello AVA. The prestige of this area provided the initial draw for the Trumps, given that "they like being best in everything." Woolard has found that for the Trumps, "location is everything, quality is everything."

Whether large-scale producers or family-run operations, location and quality are markers of many wineries in central Virginia. Picnics at Veritas Vineyards, cocktails made with Thibault-Jannison sparkling wine, the giggle-inducing labels of Well-Hung Vineyard and short ribs braised in Gabriele Rausse's Rosso are all experiences and tastes made available by the successes of Virginia's wine industry. Either for drinking by itself or for pairing with food, a bottle of wine from the Monticello AVA and nearby areas is guaranteed to have a story behind its taste, aroma and production method.

Breweries and Cideries

One can drink a glass of Virginia Fizz with two slices of cheese pizza from Christian's—the crisp acidity will help cut the salty, fatty topping—but a cold pint of beer is the more popular and likely choice. While the brewing industry of Charlottesville has not yet reached the levels of distribution and fame accorded to winemaking in the area, a reliable contingent of local brewers has appeared over the last ten years. If wine tastings and vineyard tours appeal to the Charlottesville gourmand, one who shops at Feast! and dines at the C&O, the breweries of the area draw in the festival-loving crowd, the under-thirties who choose the Whiskey Jar and hiking over crossword puzzles and Paramount concerts. The brewers are not European transplants or elegant septuagenarians but the young and the tattooed. Oyster stouts and pizza trucks, concert-friendly six packs and hot wings are the offerings of local breweries, eager to reach out to a demographic that the burgeoning wine industry has not yet enfolded.

The name "Starr Hill" has a variety of meanings to residents of Charlottesville. It can refer to the neighborhood of Charlottesville between UVA and downtown, a primarily African American area that has become more integrated recently. It can refer to the old Starr Hill brewery and concert hall, a stretching space on West Main Street that hosted the likes of They Might Be Giants and John Mayer, which closed in 2007. For most people, Starr Hill is the name of the area's largest and most successful brewery. The music-themed names and labels of Starr Hill brews, its high visibility at concerts and music venues and the foundational status of the brewery mark it as a beer to be reckoned with, a malted monolith of Trump proportions.

When Mark Thompson founded the brewery in 1999, the market was saturated with imported beer; according to Thompson, it was "a different world." Starr Hill was one of the first breweries in the commonwealth of Virginia upon taking over a spot called Blue Ridge Brewing Company. Blue Ridge Brewing Company, started by grandchildren of former UVA writer-in-residence William Faulkner in 1986, was the first brewpub in Virginia. Founded by owners who had been influenced by the German model of small hometown breweries, the brewpub was sold to Thompson, who changed the name to Starr Hill to reflect a community investment.

Not long after beginning, Starr Hill quickly became a music lifestyle brand, aided by the visibility of its West Main location and a music hall upstairs. Thompson, a charming Will Ferrell lookalike with an easy sense of humor, tells of selling T-shirts at Grateful Dead concerts, leading to entrepreneurial skills built in the parking lot. To him, "the music connection was in our DNA."[123] Starr Hill often names beers after music and song titles; some of its product offerings speak to the needs of this lifestyle, such as canned beer's usefulness for concerts and outdoor activities. Thompson finds the connection between music and alcohol to be "two and two equals five" and refers to the ties between the craft beer scene and the music scene as "a natural progression."

Starr Hill's mission statement includes the provision that "Starr Hill seeks to become the East Coast's most respected and sought-after brewery." Thompson has dreams of growing the business and becoming regional, which the brewery can accomplish by "making fresh liquid." Seasonal flavors do play into the public's conception of "fresh"; IPAs and seasonal brews, which change by the quarter, are top sellers. Thompson's research shows that consumers do like a seasonal item; winter beers are stronger, with more alcohol and a darker color. Though Thompson misses having a place for music, he doesn't miss the headaches. Starr Hill spends considerable time and effort establishing relationships with local music venues, plus Hershey Park and Raleigh. Thompson wants "to touch people with the gift of great beer."

While Starr Hill is by no means a business of Anheuser-Busch proportions, its longevity, size and successful expansion make it one of the area's largest brewing operations. Room has been left available for new operations of smaller scale to step in and fill additional niches. Thompson views the increasing number of local breweries in positive terms, noting that "a rising tide lifts all boats." The Virginia Craft Brewers Guild displays the ethos that these businesses are stronger when they band together. Each brewery has its own niche and quality; to Thompson, if the area can house two hundred wineries, there can also be room for two hundred breweries.

Hunter Smith's Champion Brewery, housed in a strip of businesses between downtown and Belmont, fills one of these niches. Tiny, inventive and highly collaborative, Champion has already distinguished itself within the past year that it has been open. Hunter Smith wanted to "get into the beer business, really ever since [he had his] first craft beer." Smith has found that his clientele is "all over the place" but are primarily "neighborhood residents or visitors to the Downtown Mall. The age varies from minimum legal drinking into middle-aged customers and older."

The variety of offerings at Champion mirrors the diversity in customers; a German-style *gose* with the name of Face Eater, a seasonal oyster stout and an 8.5 percent ABV Belgian *tripel* are all available at Champion Brewery.

Industrial beer brewing. *Photo by Kevin Haney.*

Partnerships with other local businesses, such as Blue Ridge Pizza Company, Taqueria Mi Ranchito and the Clifton Inn, keep the offerings at Champion fresh and eventful. Smith displays similar support to Mark Thompson for would-be competitors in the craft beer scene. "I think it's great that there's enough local demand for beer and wine, and it looks like local markets show strong support for growth," Smith says. "I think the number-one thing that matters is quality product. As long as the beer and wine is good and the most important thing on anyone's mind, then it's all good."

In the last several years, quality products of an alcoholic nature have begun to develop beyond wine and beer. The general interest in heritage food products, animal breeds and lifestyle choices has resulted in the resurgence of hard cider as a viable beverage option. Vintage Virginia Apples, in conjunction with Albemarle Ciderworks, has promoted education about and access to heritage varieties like the Arkansas black and the Geneva crab.[124] The joint work of Peter Hatch and Tom Burford, "a modern day Johnny Appleseed, part philosopher and part planter," at Monticello has also given root to a revival of interest in hard cider production.[125] But perhaps the greatest asset to the cider industry is the quality of the cider itself.

Absent from the offerings of Charlottesville-area cideries are the sickly sweet, overly processed varieties prevalent at chain restaurants and corner stores. Single-variety bottles, oak barrel aging and reserve blends are merely some of the marks of the new hard cider movement. Potter's Craft Cider, with its dry acidity and nuanced palate, appears at the forefront of these offerings. Reasonably priced and highly accessible, customers can choose between a 750-milliliter bottle or, in many cases, a glass of the effervescent stuff on draft at many local restaurants.

Potter's Craft Cider is a labor of love for two Princeton graduates who stumbled on a love of craft beer outside of their day jobs as a "hobby going out of control."[126] Tim Edmond, one half of the cider team along with Dan Potter, laughs when comparing his former career in finance to the work he does now at the cidery. Possessing a wealth of information about various cider-making processes, Edmond has an excitement for his new day job that's palpable in his speech and in his product.

Edmond and Potter began drawing on research, pre-Prohibition materials that hadn't been used for over one hundred years. Edmond relates that "really forward-thinking" local businesses in town were excited about their cider; Edmond states, "Cider by nature is a super-local thing. You can be a local brewery but still get hops and barley from other places; it's difficult to source local ingredients as a brewery." Edmond finds their business to be fortunately situated in this area; they picked Charlottesville for its good apples and orchardists who've been doing it for generations with heritage varieties. Other people than commercial growers are bringing back nurseries with apples that are early, such as Vintage Virginia Apples, which supplies Potter's with cider-specific apple varieties like the Hugh's crab at Monticello. Edmond characterizes these people as "forward-thinking, food-focused individuals that are very forensic about where their food comes from."

Edmond notes that unlike wine or beer, "cider has yet to emerge as its own market—are they beer drinkers? Are they wine drinkers?" The average consumer of Potter's Craft Cider has the expendable income to buy local and is interested in craft products. Edmond states that he and Potter are trying to "make that market" of craft cider drinkers, noting that there's an "established macro category of what cider is. We're trying to create that craft category." With a grassroots marketing approach and relationships with everyone from Whole Foods to Free Union Grass Farm, Edmond and Potter are quickly uncovering the nature of the customers who have made Potter's Craft Cider a household name in the area.

Wine, beer and cider from central Virginia appear on menus next to local dishes and family-recipe menus. Bottles of each dot the local retailers, whether big-box stores or gourmet grocers. The love and pride that Charlottesvillians have in their local food producers is well matched in their support of the burgeoning wine, beer and cider industries. The thread that connects all elements of food production and consumption in Charlottesville, from young farmers to locavore restaurants to Virginia wine, is the love and appreciation of fine craft and good taste—qualities that mark all aspects of local beverage production.

Notes

Introduction

1. Fearnside, "Digging In."
2. Ibid.

Chapter 1

3. City of Charlotte, "Community Profile."
4. National Oceanic and Atmospheric Administration, "NowData—NOAA Online Weather Data."
5. U.S. Census Bureau; American Community Survey, 2010, generated using "American Fact Finder," accessed October 21, 2013.
6. University of Virginia, "Human Resources."
7. Ingles, "Immigrant Story."
8. DeWitt, *Founding Foodies*.
9. Malone, "Jefferson, the Virginian," in *Jefferson and His Time*, 1:3.
10. Jefferson, "Summary of Public Service," 32:124.
11. Betts, ed., *Thomas Jefferson's Garden Book, 1766–1824*, 462.
12. Hatch, "Thomas Jefferson's Legacy in Gardening and Food."
13. Ibid.
14. Hatch, "Thomas Jefferson's Favorite Vegetables."

15. Peter Hatch in discussion with the author, May 2013.
16. Ibid.
17. Jefferson, "William Maclure to Jefferson, Paris 1801," in *Thomas Jefferson's Garden Book*, 276.
18. Jefferson, "Bernard McMahon to Jefferson, Philadelphia 1806," 328.
19. Ibid.
20. Ibid.
21. Morris, "Heritage Harvest Festival Transforms Monticello."
22. Cornett, "Jefferson's Botanical Perseverance."
23. Hatch, "Thomas Jefferson's Favorite Vegetables."
24. Ibid.
25. Rogers, "Thomas Jefferson, America's Founding Foodie."
26. Jefferson, "To Dr. Vine Utley, March 21, 1819," in *The Writings of Thomas Jefferson*, XV:187.
27. Hatch, "Thomas Jefferson's Legacy in Gardening and Food."
28. Jefferson, "To Dr. Vine Utley, March 21, 1819."
29. Thomas Jefferson Foundation, "Paris Residences."
30. Wulf, *Founding Gardeners*, 151.
31. Thomas Jefferson Foundation, "James Hemings."
32. Ibid.
33. Webster, ed., "Memorandum of Mr. Jefferson's Conversations," in *Private Correspondence of Daniel Webster*, 364–66.
34. Rogers, "Thomas Jefferson, America's Founding Foodie."
35. Jefferson, "Jefferson to Stephen Cathalan, Monticello, June 6, 1817."
36. Jefferson, *Thomas Jefferson's Garden Book*, 222.
37. Peter Hatch in discussion with the author, May 2013.
38. Lily Fox-Brugière in discussion with the author, January 2013.
39. Waters, introduction to *A Rich Spot of Earth*, xi.
40. Moser, "All the President's Produce."
41. Ibid.
42. Michie Tavern, "The Tavern's History."
43. Cindy Conte in discussion with the author, January 2013.
44. Gabriele Rausse in discussion with the author, February 2013.
45. Ibid.
46. Ibid.

CHAPTER 2

47. Virginia Department of Agriculture and Consumer Services, "Virginia Agriculture Facts and Figures."
48. Ibid.
49. Ibid.
50. Ibid.
51. Ibid.
52. Ibid., "Virginia Century Farm Program."
53. Ibid.
54. Ibid., "Virginia Agriculture Facts and Figures,"
55. Schum, "The Plain People."
56. Donnie Montgomery in discussion with the author, March 2013.
57. WSET, "Franklin Co's Homestead Creamery Receives Grant from Governor McDonnell."
58. Ibid.
59. Ibid.
60. Donnie Montgomery in discussion with the author, March 2013.
61. Ibid.
62. Benyus, *Biomimicry*, introduction.
63. Zach Miller in discussion with the author, March 2013.
64. Erica Hellen in discussion with the author, March 2013.
65. United States Department of Agriculture National Agricultural Statistics Service, "NASS Survey 2010."
66. Stanley, "Renting Farmland."
67. Seymour, *Self-Sufficient Life.*
68. Ibid.
69. London, "Permaculture: A Quiet Revolution—An Interview with Bill Mollison."
70. Ibid.
71. Owen, *Green Metropolis*, 301.
72. Pollan, "Sustaining Vision."
73. Polyface Farms, "Our Story."
74. Ibid.
75. Goodman, "Joel Salatin, America's Most Influential Farmer."
76. Ibid.
77. Ibid.
78. Gail Hobbs-Page in discussion with the author, March 2013.

CHAPTER 3

79. Talhelm, "Charlottesville Tops *Forbes*' Wealthiest & Most Charitable Lists."
80. McEvoy, "The $5 Tomato."
81. Ibid.
82. Reddy, "Sotheby's Puts Veggies on the Block."
83. Kate Collier in discussion with the author, April 2013.
84. C-VILLE writers, "Local Food Hub Linking Farm and Table in Five Counties."
85. Ibid.
86. Emily Manley in discussion with the author, May 2013.
87. Grace Communications Foundation, "Where Can You Find Sustainable Food?"
88. Zach Buckner in discussion with the author, May 2013.
89. Relay Foods, "Press Release: Relay Foods Establishes Largest Online Food Marketplace in Mid-Atlantic U.S."
90. DiMaggio, "Local Farmers Markets."
91. Provence, "Un-wreathed: City Market Founders' Kin Kicked Out."
92. Stephanie Andregg-Maloy in discussion with the author, January 2013.

CHAPTER 4

93. Satran, "Best Restaurant Cities."
94. Kurlantzick, "36 Hours in Charlottesville, Va."
95. McGowin, "Taste Charlottesville's Growing Local-Food Movement."
96. Gail Hobbs-Page in discussion with the author, March 2013.
97. Will Richey in discussion with the author, June 2013.
98. Harrison Keevil in discussion with the author, June 2013.
99. Dean Maupin in discussion with the author, June 2013.
100. Matt Rohdie in discussion with the author, June 2013.
101. Adriana Hill in discussion with the author, June 2013.
102. Donnie Montgomery in discussion with the author, June 2013.

CHAPTER 5

103. Jefferson, "Thomas Jefferson to Thomas Appleton, Monticello, 14 January 1816."
104. Jefferson, "Thomas Jefferson to John Dortie, 1811," in *Thomas Jefferson's Garden Book*, 462.
105. Ibid.
106. Monticello, "Vineyard."
107. Ibid.
108. Ibid.
109. Ibid.
110. Ireland, "Barboursville Wine Slated for Chinese Import."
111. Apple, "Jefferson Gets His Wish."
112. Ibid.
113. Ibid.
114. Luca Paschina in discussion with the author, July 2013.
115. Apple, "Jefferson Gets His Wish."
116. Brashear, "Growing Good Wine in Virginia's Unlikely Clime."
117. Gabriele Rausse in discussion with the author, February 2013.
118. Margaux and Company, "Gabriele Rausse."
119. Ibid.
120. Burrus, "A Vintner's Vintner."
121. Berninger, "Vines and Wines: Trump Winery's 2007 SP Reserve."
122. Kerry Woolard in discussion with the author, March 2013.
123. Mark Thompson in discussion with the author, May 2013.
124. Vintage Virginia Apples, "Apple Varieties."
125. Morris, "Professor Apple."
126. Tim Edmond in conversation with the author, May 2013.

Bibliography

Apple, R.W., Jr. "Jefferson Gets His Wish: At Last, a Decent Bottle of Virginia Wine." *New York Times*, September 13, 2000. http://www.nytimes.com/2000/09/13/dining/jefferson-gets-his-wish-at-last-a-decent-bottle-of-virginia-wine.html?pagewanted=all&src=pm (accessed November 1, 2013).

Benyus, Janine. *Biomimicry: Innovation Inspired by Nature*. New York: Perennial, 1997.

Berninger, Jack. "Vines and Wines: Trump Winery's 2007 SP Reserve." *Richmond Times-Dispatch*, March 24, 2013. http://www.timesdispatch.com/entertainment-life/columnists-blogs/jack-berninger/vines-and-wines-trump-winery-s-sp-reserve/article_4bc1f4b4-fa34-523a-a530-5c63817c15b2.html (accessed November 2, 2013).

Betts, Edwin M., ed. *Thomas Jefferson's Garden Book, 1766–1824: With Relevant Extracts from His Other Writings*. Charlottesville: University of Virginia Press, 1999.

Brashear, Graelyn. "Growing Good Wine in Virginia's Unlikely Clime." *C-VILLE Weekly*, September 12, 2012. http://www.c-ville.com/growing-good-wine-in-virginias-unlikely-clime/#.UncVOpSpsrU (accessed November 1, 2013).

Burrus, Mary. "A Vintner's Vintner." *Virginia Living*, October 2011. http://www.virginialiving.com/food-drink/a-vintners-vintner (accessed November 2, 2013).

City of Charlottesville. "Community Profile." Charlottesville City Website. http://www.charlottesville.org/Index.aspx?page=154 (accessed October 21, 2013).

Cornett, Peggy. "Jefferson's Botanical Perseverance." *Twinleaf Journal Online*, 1995. http://www.monticello.org/site/house-and-gardens/jeffersons-botanical-perseverance.

C-VILLE writers. "Local Food Hub Linking Farm and Table in Five Counties." *C-VILLE Weekly*, July 14, 2009. http://www.c-ville.com/Local_Food_Hub_linking_farm_and_table_in_five_counties/ (accessed October 22, 2013).

DeWitt, Dave. *The Founding Foodies: How Washington, Jefferson, and Franklin Revolutionized American Cuisine.* Chicago: Sourcebooks, 2010.

DiMaggio, Joanne. "Local Farmers Markets." *C-VILLE Weekly*, June 14, 2012. http://www.c-ville.com/span_classApple_style_span_stylefont_family_Verdana_Arial_sans_serif_font_size_12pxstrongLocal_Farmers_Marketsstrongspan/#.UmiKdpSpsjR (accessed October 22, 2013).

Fearnside, Jeffrey. "Digging In: Wendell Berry on Small Farms, Local Wisdom, and the Folly of Greed." *The Sun*, July 2008. http://thesunmagazine.org/issues/391/digging_in (accessed November 4, 2013).

Goodman, Makenna. "Joel Salatin, America's Most Influential Farmer, Talks Big Organic and the Future of Food." Treehugger website, August 5, 2009. http://www.treehugger.com/green-food/joel-salatin-americas-most-influential-farmer-talks-big-organic-and-the-future-of-food.html (accessed October 22, 2013).

Grace Communications Foundation. "Where Can You Find Sustainable Food?" Grace Communications Foundations website. http://www.sustainabletable.org/566/where-can-you-find-sustainable-food (accessed October 22, 2013).

Hatch, Peter J. "Thomas Jefferson's Favorite Vegetables." *Twinleaf Journal Online*, 2000. http://www.monticello.org/site/house-and-gardens/thomas-jeffersons-favorite-vegetables (accessed October 21, 2013).

———. "Thomas Jefferson's Legacy in Gardening and Food." *Twinleaf Journal Online*, 2010. http://www.monticello.org/site/house-and-gardens/thomas-jeffersons-legacy-gardening-and-food (accessed October 21, 2013).

Ingles, Laura. "Immigrant Story: IRC Relocates Hundreds of Refugees to Charlottesville Each Year." *C-Ville Weekly*, February 5, 2010. http://www.c-ville.com/charlottesville-gets-a-multicultural-facelift-as-irc-relocates-hundreds-of-refugees-each-year/#.UmV5V5SpsjQ (accessed October 21, 2013).

Ireland, Casey. "Barboursville Wine Slated for Chinese Import." *C-VILLE Weekly*, August 3, 2011. http://www.c-ville.com/Barboursville_wine_slated_for_Chinese_import/#.UncGP5SpsrU (accessed November 2, 2013).

Jefferson, Thomas. "Jefferson to Stephen Cathalan, Monticello, June 6, 1817." Washington, D.C.: Library of Congress.

———. "Summary of Public Service." *The Papers of Thomas Jefferson*. Edited by Julian P. Boyd, Charles T. Cullen, John Catanzariti, Barbara B. Oberg, et al. Princeton, NJ: Princeton University Press, 1950.

———. *Thomas Jefferson's Garden Book*. Edited by Peter J. Hatch. Chapel Hill: University of North Carolina Press, 1999.

———. "Thomas Jefferson to Thomas Appleton, Monticello, 14 January 1816." Washington, D.C.: Library of Congress.

———. *The Writings of Thomas Jefferson*. Edited by Andrew Lipscomb. Volume XV. Washington, D.C.: Thomas Jefferson Memorial Association, 1903.

Kurlantzick, Joshua. "36 Hours in Charlottesville, Va." *New York Times*, October 23, 2008. http://www.nytimes.com/2008/10/26/travel/26hours.html?pagewanted=all (accessed October 25, 2013).

London, Scott. "Permaculture: A Quiet Revolution—An Interview with Bill Mollison." http://www.scottlondon.com/interviews/mollison.html (accessed October 22, 2013).

Malone, Dumas. "Jefferson, the Virginian," in *Jefferson and His Time*. Vol 1. New York: Little, Brown, 1948.

Margaux and Company. "Gabriele Rausse." http://www.margauxandcompany.com/portfolio.php?pro=69 (accessed November 2, 2013).

McEvoy, Meg. "The $5 Tomato." *C-VILLE Weekly*, July 31, 2006. http://www.c-ville.com/The_5_tomato/#.UmiEW5SpsjQ (accessed October 22, 2013).

McGowin, Warner. "Taste Charlottesville's Growing Local-Food Movement." *Southern Living Magazine*, 2009. http://www.southernliving.com/travel/south-east/charlottesville-virginia-organic-farms-00400000049579/page9.html (accessed October 25, 2013).

Michie Tavern. "The Tavern's History." http://www.michietavern.com/the-tavern-history/ (accessed October 21, 2013).

Monticello. "Vineyard." http://www.monticello.org/site/house-and-gardens/vineyard (accessed November 2, 2013).

Morris, Giles. "Heritage Harvest Festival Transforms Monticello into Celebration of Farm Culture." *C-Ville Weekly*, September 11, 2012. http://www.c-ville.com/heritage-harvest-festival-transforms-monticello/ (accessed October 21, 2013).

———. "Professor Apple: How Tom Burford Sowed the Seeds of the Virginia Hard Cider Revival." *C-VILLE Weekly*, November 9, 2012. http://www.c-ville.com/virginia-hard-cider-revival/#.UndFL5SpsrU (accessed November 2, 2013).

Moser, Laura. "All the President's Produce." *Wall Street Journal*, April 27, 2012. http://online.wsj.com/news/articles/SB10001424052702303592404577362284112772226 (accessed October 21, 2013).

National Oceanic and Atmospheric Administration. "NowData—NOAA Online Weather Data." http://www.nws.noaa.gov/climate/xmacis.php?wfo=lwx (accessed October 21, 2013).

Owen, David. *Green Metropolis*. New York: Riverhead, 2009.

Pollan, Michael. "Sustaining Vision." *Gourmet Magazine*, August 31, 2002. http://michaelpollan.com/articles-archive/sustaining-vision/ (accessed October 22, 2013).

Polyface Farms. "Our Story." http://www.polyfacefarms.com/story/ (accessed October 22, 2013).

Provence, Lisa. "Un-wreathed: City Market Founders' Kin Kicked Out." *The Hook*, November 16, 2010. http://www.readthehook.com/66016/un-wreathed-city-market-founders-kin-kicked-out (accessed October 22, 2013).

Reddy, Sumathi. "Sotheby's Puts Veggies on the Block." *Wall Street Journal*, August 14, 2010. http://online.wsj.com/news/articles/SB10001424052748703960004575427433671986168#project=SLIDESHOW08&s=SB10001424052748703960004575427690714369922&articleTabs=article (accessed October 22, 2013).

Relay Foods. "Press Release: Relay Foods Establishes Largest Online Food Marketplace in Mid-Atlantic U.S." August 28, 2012. http://blog.relayfoods.com/press-release-relay-foods-establishes-largest-online-food-marketplace-in-mid-atlantic-u-s/ (accessed October 22, 2013).

Rogers, Felisa. "Thomas Jefferson, America's Founding Foodie." *Salon*, July 2, 2011. http://www.salon.com/2011/07/02/jefferson_culinary_history/ (accessed October 21, 2013).

Satran, Joe. "Best Restaurant Cities: 15 U.S. Metro Areas with the Most Eateries Per Capita." *Huffington Post*, January 25, 2013. http://www.huffingtonpost.com/2013/01/25/best-restaurant-cities_n_2545499.html#slide=2023417 (accessed October 25, 2013).

Schum, Guy. "The Plain People." *Virginia Living*, February 2012. http://www.virginialiving.com/exploring/the-plain-people/ (accessed October 22, 2013).

Seymour, John. *The Self-Sufficient Life and How to Live It*. London: Dorling Kindersley, 2003. Publisher's release.

Stanley, Tom. "Renting Farmland." Virginia Cooperative Extension website, August 1, 2009. http://pubs.ext.vt.edu/news/fbmu/2009/04/RentingFarmLand.html (accessed October 23, 2013).

Talhelm, Matt. "Charlottesville Tops *Forbes*' Wealthiest & Most Charitable Lists." September 20, 2011. http://www.nbc29.com/story/15509016/charlottesville-ranks-as-one-of-wealthiest-most-charitable (accessed October 20, 2013).

Thomas Jefferson Foundation. "James Hemings." http://www.monticello.org/site/plantation-and-slavery/james-hemings (accessed October 21, 2013).

———. "Paris Residences." http://www.monticello.org/site/research-and-collections/paris-residences (accessed October 21, 2013).

University of Virginia. "Human Resources." http://www.hr.virginia.edu/hr-for-you/prospective-employees/jobs/ (accessed October 21, 2013).

U.S. Census Bureau. "American Community Survey, 2010." Generated using "American Fact Finder." http://factfinder2.census.gov/faces/nav/jsf/pages/community_facts.xhtml (accessed October 21, 2013).

U.S. Department of Agriculture National Agricultural Statistics Service. "NASS Survey 2010." http://charlottesvillefarmsandland.com/index.php/2011/11/leasing-out-your-farm/ (accessed October 22, 2013).

Vintage Virginia Apples. "Apple Varieties." http://www.albemarleciderworks.com/orchard/apple-varieties (accessed November 2, 2013).

Virginia Department of Agriculture and Consumer Services. "Virginia Agriculture Facts and Figures." http://www.vdacs.virginia.gov/agfacts/index.shtml (accessed October 22, 2013).

———. "Virginia Century Farm Program." http://www.vdacs.virginia.gov/century/ (accessed October 22, 2013).

Waters, Alice. "Introduction." In *A Rich Spot of Earth*, by Peter J. Hatch, xi. New Haven, CT: Yale University Press, 2012.

Webster, Fletcher, ed. "Memorandum of Mr. Jefferson's Conversations." In *Private Correspondence of Daniel Webster*. Boston: 1857.

WSET. "Franklin Co's Homestead Creamery Receives Grant from Governor McDonnell." December 17, 2012. http://www.wset.com/story/20366487/franklin-cos-homestead-creamery-recieves-grant-from-governor-mcdonnell (accessed October 22, 2013).

Wulf, Andrea. *Founding Gardeners*. New York: Vintage, 2011.

About the Author

Casey Ireland is a Virginia native and a resident of Charlottesville since 2008. She received her master's degree in English literature from the University of Virginia in 2013. Along with writing food reviews and papers on medieval English literature, Casey enjoys eating and cooking—preferably with friends and family. This is her first book.

Photo by Kevin Haney.

Visit us at
www.historypress.net

This title is also available as an e-book